UP FOR GRABS

Inquiries into Who Wants What

DANIEL JACK CHASAN

Madrona Publishers, Inc.   ·   Seattle

Library of Congress Cataloging in Publication Data

Chasan, Daniel Jack.
     Up for grabs.

     Includes index.
     1. Environmental policy—United States.
2. Conservation of natural resources—United
States.   I. Title.
HC110.E5C47   333.7′0973   77-23881
ISBN 0-914842-18-8
ISBN 0-914842-17-X pbk.

Portions of chapters 2 and 5 appeared originally
in *Audubon*. Other material in the book has been
published in *Pacific Search*.

Madrona Publishers, Inc.
113 Madrona Place East
Seattle, Washington 98112

For Esther and for Will

Contents

UP FOR GRABS

Inquiries into Who Wants What

1. The Last Tree

Not long ago, a friend of mine talked with an old man who claimed to have cut down the very last big virgin Douglas fir on Vashon Island, where I live. The tree was some two hundred feet tall, the old man said, and it rose one hundred feet before the straight sweep of the trunk was broken by the first branches. It was a good thirteen feet across at the base. Much of the island is still covered with trees, but not trees like that. My friend had an acquaintance in the forest products industry do a little quick calculating, and found that there had probably been enough good lumber in that tree to frame twelve houses. But the old man hadn't cut it for lumber to build houses. He had cut the last big virgin Douglas fir on Vashon Island for firewood. It made good firewood, too. He burned it in his iron stove for ten years.

It seems absurd, from a later perspective, to have cut that tree for firewood. The man probably had little money at the time—it was the Depression—and could certainly be forgiven the desire to keep himself and his family warm. But it was a disaster. If you think of the tree as a tree, it was an aesthetic and environmental disaster. If you think of the tree as lumber in the raw, it was an economic disaster.

However you think of the tree, the fact remains that it was

on the old man's land, so it was his tree. If he wanted to cut it for firewood, he had that right.

This story may or may not be true in any or all of its particulars. I don't know. And in a way, it doesn't matter. True or not, the story is entirely plausible. Similar things have been happening for centuries. Similar things happen today.

Ownership of, or the right to use trees or land, fish or water virtually always confers the right to make those resources unusable for other purposes or by other people. Sometimes it confers a right to simply destroy them.

For example, I have a perfect right to fell all the big cedars that grow in and around the swamp behind our house. Those trees are at least two hundred years old, and mature red cedars are definitely a vanishing species, but all that is irrelevant. I could split the trees into shakes and sell them for $45 a square. I could cut them into two-foot-by-six-inch logs and burn them in our iron stove. Or I could just leave them on the forest floor. It is my choice.

To make such a choice is a conventional prerogative of ownership. If I owned more land or different land, my prerogatives might be even grander. Instead of two-hundred-year-old cedars, I might, for example, be able to obliterate thousand-year-old sequoias. It was necessary to create a Redwoods National Park in 1968 because, despite the historic, symbolic, elementary-textbook-picture place that redwoods occupy in this country, redwoods on private land are simply so much standing timber, and they were being cut at a rapid clip. A few more years, and many of the big ones would have been gone. The lumber industry is still logging giant redwoods around the periphery of the national park. And why not? The companies have an investment there, they are responsible to their shareholders, not to posterity.

Today, the fate not only of the forests but of many resources on which the future of this country may depend is bound up inextricably with questions of ownership and control.

Private ownership does not necessarily guarantee the worst possible use of those resources. For some of the inhabitants of North America, it has often been less of a curse than public ownership. No individual owned the buffalo. No individual owned the passenger pigeon. And no individual has owned the salmon, either. In each of those cases and many more, what happened can be described as everybody-owns-it-so-nobody-owns-it-so-everyone-should-grab-what-he-can. One is not likely to make sacrifices or even try very hard to conserve that on which one has no special claim. (This is not a recent discovery. In February of 1810, Thomas Jefferson wrote from Monticello, "We have had the most devastating rain which has ever fallen within my knowledge. Three inches of water fell in the space of about an hour. Every hollow of every hill presented a torrent which swept everything before it. I have never seen the fields so much injured. Mr. Randolph's farm is the only one which has not suffered; his horizontal furrows arrested the water at every step till it was absorbed, or at least had deposited the soil it had taken up. Everybody in this neighborhood is adopting his method of ploughing, except [the] tenants, who have no interest in the preservation of the soil.")

Once, much of the United States was covered with huge virgin trees. Virtually all of those trees were cut decades or centuries ago by people who owned them, and by people who had a right to cut them because no one or everyone owned them.

We are often reminded that Theodore Roosevelt once defined conservation as the "wise use" of resources. Everyone thinks he or she wants to use a given resource wisely. But what looks like wisdom to the Sierra Club may look like folly to the forest products industry, and vice versa. Clearly, there are people who resent the loss of any tree in any forest. Clearly, they are not the people who earn a living by logging, working in lumber or pulp mills, loading forest products onto ships or building frame houses. Nor are they the executives of construction or forest products companies. Whose definition of wisdom applies? Who gets to benefit from the resource's use? Who gets to decide who benefits?

Each society will work out its own answers to these questions. Each will have its own range of answers derived from its specific culture and economy. But the questions apply in every society. We in the United States confront such questions not because we have inherited European culture or the capitalist system, but because we have inherited human nature. Since the start of the environmental movement, writers have contrasted the greedy, materialistic West with Native American culture. The Indians did not believe in unlimited economic growth, we are told. They were the "first conservationists." They had a reverence for nature and all its creatures. For many of them, the very idea of owning land was repellent.

That is all true enough. But in practical terms, what does it mean? Faced with limited markets in a subsistence or barter economy, the Indians refrained from killing or harvesting more than they could use. Living as hunters and gatherers, they did not feel compelled to plow or subdivide the soil.

It is true that the Indians of the Northwest, for example, didn't believe in ownership of land, but the ownership of land had no economic value to them. Prime fishing spots did have economic value to them, and among the Yakimas who lived beside the Columbia River, prime fishing spots could not only be owned, they could be passed on from generation to generation.

Farther south, where the Aztecs and their neighbors practiced a highly-developed agriculture based in part on the laboriously-created artificial islands called *chinampas,* land was definitely owned. Ultimately, all land was owned by the tribe, which divided it among the clans, which divided it among the individual families. A single family holding could be passed on from father to son. In an agricultural society, Indian or not, the ownership of land has economic value.

Today, all of our forests and valleys and bodies of water have economic value (often, they have many conflicting economic values, as well as other values that conflict with conventional economics) and people have consequently tried to stake claims to all of them.

If a resource is obviously limited, society will establish an order of precedence for using it. If the resource itself is perceived as being unlimited, but the best points of access to it are scarce—as with the Yakimas' fishing spots—society will establish an order of precedence for using *them*. This will happen even if the resource itself is truly inexhaustible. It has been suggested—by both large energy companies and legal scholars—that as the solar heating and cooling of buildings comes into widespread use, the owners of adjacent high-rises will get drawn into sharp, complex legal conflicts over access to sunlight. "Land with good southern exposure . . . [will] be enhanced in value," General Electric suggested in a 1974 report. ". . . Legislative action to resolve questions of sun rights and the authority of local governments to engage in three-dimensional zoning will be necessary."

Creating orders of precedence for the use of limited resources or access points is not a uniquely human activity. It is an activity that human beings share with their relatives, the monkeys and apes. All or virtually all monkeys can climb, but they do not all spend identical amounts of time in the trees. Some are fundamentally tree dwellers, while others spend most of their time on the ground. Among the ground dwellers, there is almost always a rigid hierarchy in which the older, stronger monkeys get first crack at the food, the slightly weaker monkeys get second crack, and so on. Among the tree dwellers, there is generally no such hierarchy.

So far as anyone knows, the reason for this sharp difference in social organization lies in the abundance in which food is most likely to be found by the two types of monkeys. A group of tree-dwelling monkeys will come upon fruit or nuts by the treeful. In a single large tree, there will usually be enough for everyone, and there is no reason for some monkeys to crowd the others out. Ground dwellers, on the other hand, will be more likely to come upon fruit or nuts in relatively small piles, so that not all the monkeys can partake at the same time. If a group of normally tree-dwelling monkeys is placed in a situation in which food can be obtained only one piece at a time—as in an experiment with Diana monkeys at the Portland, Oregon zoo—they develop an order of precedence, too. It would seem to be the availability or scarcity of food at any given place and time that leads monkeys to develop strict rules of precedence.

It is possible to interpret a good deal of human history as an attempt by presumably civilized nations of human beings to develop rather similar orders of precedence for the use of natural resources. Europe's colonization of the Americas, its struggle for colonies before World War I, Japan's expansionism of the 1930s—the list of historical examples can be extended indefinitely.

For a while, in portions of the industrialized world, access to resources was taken very much for granted. Technology was capturing the world's imagination and absorbing a lot of its creative energy. Resources were just there.

That attitude toward resources has not survived the early 1970s, and the evidence of its demise is hard to miss. It is inconceivable, for example, that any modern industrial nation would waste five minutes on the opinions, wishes or aspirations of a handful of sparsely populated, inconveniently located and autocratically governed states in the Middle Eastern deserts if those states didn't happen to be sitting on top of much of the world's known supply of a finite and extremely valuable resource: petroleum. The current significance of petroleum may be the most obvious example, but it is not the only one. In the cold ocean waters around Iceland, European nations have been competing not for oil but for fish. Both Icelandic and British fishermen have been catching North

Atlantic cod practically forever. In the early 1970s, Icelandic gunboats started cutting the trawl lines of British boats fishing within fifty miles of Iceland's coast, and a shell was fired into the engine room of one British boat. British frigates went out to protect the trawlers. There were incidents day in and day out. Finally, in early 1976, Iceland broke diplomatic relations with Britain. If Iceland and Britain can sever relations over the right to catch codfish in a particular place, access to resources has regained its overt importance.

The United States does not have all the natural resources which its economy needs. No developed nation does. But the United States does possess some resources in spectacular abundance; they include fertile soil, fresh water, forests and fish.

The agricultural scientist Georg Borgstrom has devoted much of his book, *Too Many,* to pointing out that even in an age of space exploration, those are exactly the resources on which the world's ability to feed itself still depends. The value of the United States' agricultural and forest exports far exceeds the value of its petroleum imports from the Middle East. American grain exports, which doubled during the early 1970s, already constitute a source of international economic leverage. There is no reason to believe that the significance of agricultural exports will wane in the foreseeable future.

Lester R. Brown, president of the Worldwatch Institute, wrote in the December 12, 1975, issue of *Science* that "the scarcity of basic resources required to expand food output, the negative ecological trends that are gaining momentum year by year in the poor countries, and the diminishing returns on the use of energy and fertilizer in agriculture in the industrial countries lead me to conclude that a world of cheap, abundant food . . . may now be history. In the future, scarcity may be more or less persistent, relieved only by sporadic surpluses of a local and short-lived nature. The prospects are that dependence on North America will . . . continue to increase. . . ."

The resources of land and water that first nurtured the Pilgrims in their "hideous and desolate wilderness," that gave Jefferson his hope for a nation of yeoman farmers, seem to be among the greatest assets that America takes into its third century. Used prudently, they will last forever. Used imprudently, they will be destroyed or vastly diminished. Their use will determine patterns of economic development: the distribution of jobs and derivative industries, the placement of transportation systems, the growth or restriction of population centers.

To find out what will happen to those resources, and what will consequently happen to the physical and economic shape of the United States, one might well start by asking, "who owns it?" To what extent and under what circumstances can a given resource be manipulated by this nation or, within this nation, by a single well-defined group? At what point does one type of economic use drive out or diminish the importance of another? Even assuming a resource is ostensibly public, can an individual or corporation gain the legal right to determine its future? Can an individual or corporation gain the *de facto* power to determine its future? Can society, in the form of the state, protect one use from the impact of another? Can society, in the form of the state, actually choose among uses or users?

Those questions may seem obvious to the point of simplemindedness, but after discussing them with a number of intelligent people, I have the impression that in practice they seldom come to mind. People tend to frame an issue in terms of a resource *per se* or the economy of a particular region, to pigeonhole it as an "energy" issue or an "environmental" issue. The underlying questions of ownership and control tend to get lost in the shuffle. Yet the questions of ownership and control are always there. By pursuing them, one can analyze many disparate conflicts in similar terms. One can find similarities between the historical conflicts over salmon in the North Pacific and water in the arid West, between the efforts to save agricultural land near cities and to alter logging practices in the National Forests.

Lines of ownership and control do not create absolute distinctions between good guys and bad guys. They do have a lot to do with the way things work. Obviously, if you want to know what will happen to a given resource, you must know who has the right or power to use it, and in what ways. If you want to alter the fate of a resource, you must alter the ways in which it can be used, or must forbid certain people to use it.

The point is not that every aspect of human society must be viewed in economic terms. But all conflicts over natural resources must be. What, after all, *is* a natural resource? It is a part of nature that has been assigned an economic value. It has been incorporated into an economic system. It has become a commodity. To discuss resources without considering economics would be like discussing pornography without considering sex; one could presumably do it, but one would seem to be missing the point.

2. Pacific Salmon: Fishing for Money

THE two commercial salmon fishermen were sitting at a formica-topped table in a dockside restaurant, looking out through plate-glass windows at fishing boats tied up at the dock or pulled up out of the water for repairs. "I'm not going to Alaska this year," one said. "It's the first time in twenty years, but it's just not worth it." He went on to explain that there were no longer enough fish to go around; the big fish runs had disappeared because "the Japs have caught them all." The other observed that the Japanese "are very unscrupulous people. What they're doing isn't against international law, but it's morally wrong, like somebody else harvesting your crop. It's as if they came over here and cut our timber."

How can anyone feel so possessive about a fish—not a fish wrapped in newspaper or lying in a refrigerated hold, but a fish swimming freely in the ocean, a salmon in the Bering Sea, a haddock in the mid-Atlantic, a tuna west of Guayaquil? The most obvious answer is that people feel possessive about resources that are found near, as well as on, their own turf. A second answer is that, as in the case of salmon, people feel possessive about resources that originate on their turf. A third is that people feel possessive not only about the resources themselves, but also about the opportunity to exploit them. The psychological leap from we-have-a-right-to-exploit-it-because-it's-in-our-backyard, to we-have-a-right-to-exploit-it-because-we've-been-exploiting-it-for-years isn't long.

A final answer is simply that, whatever the reason, fish in the open sea evoke strong and often conflicting feelings of possessiveness all over the world. In fact, anyone seeking a case study of human possessiveness on an international scale should probably look first at the modern history of a single fish, the Pacific salmon.

Salmon are spawned and spend their early lives in fresh-water streams, often many miles from the sea. After varying periods of time, they swim downstream to salt water, where they put on most of their adult weight and often travel thousands of miles, crossing and re-crossing national boundaries. When the fish are fully mature, they return en masse, at predictable times, to the mouths of the rivers and streams from which they entered the sea. They swim upstream to the spots where they themselves were spawned, lay and fertilize their eggs, then die. Because they spend so much time and swim so far in salt water, they can easily be regarded as international property. Because they are spawned and live parts of their lives between banks of solid ground, they can just as easily be regarded as the rightful property of a single nation.

If comparable numbers of hake or rock cod followed the salmon's migration routes through the North Pacific, the chances are that no one would get terribly upset. But the salmon is an extremely valuable fish—a single sockeye or red salmon is worth around five dollars—and salmon fishing is a perfect illustration of Edward Wenk, Jr.'s observation in *The Politics of the Ocean* that "people don't go to sea to fish for fish, they go to sea to fish for money." A tuna-sized can of salmon in an American supermarket will probably set you back at least two dollars. At that price, the starving masses of the Third World can hardly hope to afford it and neither, for that matter, can the less affluent citizens of the industrialized world.

Even the catching of fish less valuable than salmon is generally of little benefit to the truly starving nations of the world. Noting that "currently, five nations are catching approximately 50 per cent of the total 69-million-ton world fish catch," Wenk wrote that, "the species sought are those of high market value, and those fishery products involved in world trade are primarily consumed by the more affluent who have less need for the protein essence." The nations with the capacity to catch a lot of fish don't exercise that capacity in order to keep the wolf from their own doors. They exercise it to keep their bank accounts full, to provide feed and fertilizer for more profitable food industries, to nourish their people not adequately but well. Georg Borgstrom wrote in the July 1976 issue of *Smithsonian* that after World War Two, "the fishing nations prided themselves on far outstripping agriculture in the production race (the average annual increase in the catch from 1950 to 1975 was 5 per cent). More than two-thirds of the catch ended up among the well-fed, with about a third being converted to meal and oil. . . . Several European countries put more fish protein . . . into animal production than into human food. . . ."

Despite all the serious talk and speculation that the earth's inability to feed its growing population must inevitably lead to war, the fact is that the rich and powerful nations are not the hungry nations, and their rivalries do not have much to do with food *per se*. This does not jibe well with the argument that poverty is the cause of wars, but that argument has always been tenuous at best. Big wars are not started by scrawny, ninety-eight-pound nations who are tired of having sand kicked in their faces; big wars are started by muscular nations who want a larger share of the beach. If food really does become *the* vital resource of the future, it is not likely to lead to major conflicts between the scrawny and the well-fed—unless, of course, the further proliferation of nuclear weapons eventually provides even the scrawniest nation, in effect, with its own .45. For the time being, if one speaks of international conflicts over fish, one is generally talking about conflicts over a commodity, not over the next meal.

All things considered, it isn't hard to see why salmon have long provoked more than their share of such conflicts, or why the more commercially valuable the species of salmon, the more bitter and enduring the conflict is likely to be. Because the red flesh of the sockeye looks particularly nice in cans, it has long been the most commercially attractive species of all. It was sockeye that those fishermen in the restaurant were most concerned about. And not long before their conversation occurred, William Egan, then governor of Alaska, had threatened to seal off the sockeye run of Bristol Bay and let Alaskans wipe out the most valuable salmon fishery in the world if fishermen from Japan and the Pacific Northwest didn't leave the sockeye alone.

Predictably, Governor Egan's threat (which was never taken seriously even by the Alaskan press except as a reflection of the way many people felt) and decades of grumbling by American fishermen have done little or nothing to resolve the long-standing disputes over Pacific salmon. Less predictably, neither have the various sessions of the Law of the Sea Conference, and neither has the imposition by the United States of a 200-mile zone of economic control. For many fishermen, "the 200-mile limit is like motherhood," observed William Saletic, former executive director of the Purse Seine Vessel Owners' Association, not long after his return from the 1974 Law of the Sea Conference session in Caracas. "It's a very emotional issue. But I hear fishermen talking about the 200-mile limit and they don't know what the hell they're talking about. For salmon, a 200-mile limit won't do a damn bit of good."

It isn't hard to see why the 200-mile limit became a moth-

erhood issue for American coastal fishermen. In appearance
and effect, the establishment of a 200-mile limit is a classic
colonial gesture, an extension of national power to a place
beyond the nation's traditional boundaries. It is a case of national wish fulfillment—I want therefore I own—a grab of
impressive dimensions. But in intent, the 200-mile limit is
less a grab than an attempt to keep others from grabbing.
The impulse behind it is classically anti-colonial, a defensive
reflex by a nation that sees its resources being gobbled up by
foreigners with whom it is ill-equipped to compete.

Viewed that way, the United States' decision to establish a
200-mile limit of its own marks a real historical turning point.
It is no longer only the banana republics—or anchovy republics, if you prefer—that want to keep the big, rich foreigners
from catching their fish.

What American fishermen on both the Atlantic and Pacific
Coasts have resented is not the presence of small Russian,
East European and Japanese boats in their own traditional
fishing grounds, but the presence of *big* Russian, East European and Japanese boats that fish around the clock and
dwarf their own efforts and accomplishments. American
coastal fishing is, by and large, carried out by individual
small entrepreneurs in small boats. It is in many respects an
admirable system, preserving individual enterprise, self-
reliance, personal freedom. The United States government
has encouraged it, and it remains economically significant to
the states of both coasts. It is not economically efficient, however—economists have speculated that if one figures in all
the costs, American coastal fishing actually operates at a
loss—and if it encounters a heavily capitalized, heavily mechanized state or corporate-owned fleet, it can't compete.
One of the few types of fishing on which the Americans lav-
ish heavy capital investment and sophisticated equipment is
tuna fishing. It was to fend off the big, sophisticated, expensive North American tuna boats that South American nations
originated the idea of a 200-mile limit.

A portion of nature becomes a resource only when someone has the means to exploit it. To exploit a resource like undersea minerals, one needs advanced technology and a lot of money. To exploit fish, one needs virtually nothing. Everyone can catch fish. Fishing can be done with relatively—or absolutely—primitive equipment, operated or organized in a relatively—or absolutely—primitive way. But not all methods of fishing will be equally productive. In general, the more complex and capital-intensive method will be more productive than the less. (It will also pose a greater long-term danger to the fish.) In an otherwise equal competition between the two, the less highly capitalized method is likely to come out the loser. The people who employ it will naturally be resentful, and will want some kind of protection.

The world-wide establishment of 200-mile zones of economic control will end most conflicts over coastal fishing—or at least, will end them if the nations which impose such limits can figure out how to enforce them, or if other fishing nations are willing to go along.

Pacific salmon, which according to a booklet passed out by the American delegation at Caracas "support a larger number of fishermen, vessels and boats and canneries than any other North American fishery," present a thornier problem. Most of the world's great fishing grounds lie within 50 miles or so of shore, but many salmon swim out beyond even a 200-mile limit. Closer to shore, the salmon that have been spawned in one country are not aware of the boundaries of the country next door.

Along the Pacific Northwest coast, the United States and Canada share two borders and a jumble of islands and straits. Both nations harbor many salmon fishermen and many salmon, and deciding where the former may catch the latter has not been easy. Historically, it has been particularly hard in the case of the Fraser River salmon.

The Fraser, which reaches salt water near Vancouver, British Columbia, produces more sockeye than any other single river system in the world. It flows entirely through Canadian territory, and its tributary streams in which the salmon spawn are all in Canadian territory, too. But the main pathway from the mouth of the Fraser to the open Pacific leads past the American promontories of Point Roberts and Cape Flattery and through the San Juan Islands, some of which belong to the United States.

During the late nineteenth century, enterprising Americans set up fish traps—big funnels of nets supported by floating wooden platforms—along Point Roberts and the more strategically located San Juan Islands. Equally enterprising but less wealthy Americans settled for intercepting Fraser River salmon with small boats and nets. By the 1890s, fishermen from both the United States and Canada were preying extensively on the Fraser River runs.

Before the century ended, the Canadians had developed a distinct feeling that something was wrong. Ostensibly, and with some justification, they were concerned about the biological survival of the salmon. No doubt they were equally concerned about the fact that more than half of the fish were being caught by residents of the United States. (An American government salmon expert has observed that traditionally, for all nations concerned, " 'conservation' just meant that *you* wanted the fish.") An international commission was formed in 1908 to study the condition of the Fraser River runs. The following year, it recommended a two-day closed period every week during the fishing season and regulation of fish traps and boats. Canada said it would incorporate the recommendations into its fishing laws immediately, once the international agreement was ratified. But the United States, despite a plea several years later by President Woodrow Wilson, would not adopt the recommendations. The state of Washington, whose fishermen were taking most of the Fraser River catch, did not want any restrictions placed on them, and Congress refused to override its wishes.

By the end of World War I, it was obvious that the Fraser River salmon, as well as the Canadian fishermen, were really in trouble. In 1913, the blasting for a railroad construction project in Hell's Gate Canyon, a hundred miles northeast of Vancouver, had created a massive rockslide that blocked part of the Fraser to salmon swimming upstream and drastically reduced the size of the salmon runs. High wartime prices had stimulated more intensive salmon fishing than ever before, further depopulating the river. Another international commission was set up in 1917, and it made recommendations similar to those of 1909. Again the Canadians indicated that they would accept the proposals, and again the United States Senate refused. Evidently using logic familiar to the parents of many five-year-olds, Washington State preferred the bigger share of a small pie to an equal share of a large one.

Negotiators for the two nations finally managed to sign a treaty in Washington, D.C. in 1929, but there was still many a slip between signing and congressional approval. The treaty, which established an International Pacific Salmon Fisheries Commission, proclaimed, "It is agreed by the high contracting parties that they should share equally in the fishing." Washington State had been raking in a full two-thirds of the catch since 1906, so sharing equally did not appeal to the state's elected officials. They made the treaty an issue of states' rights, and the U.S. Senate was still unwilling to interfere.

Then in 1935, everything changed. Washington fishermen had been catching many of the Fraser River salmon in fish traps. A single trap could catch far more salmon and make its owner far more money than several small fishing boats. But the traps were expensive to build, the number of places suitable for building them was limited, and in practice they were monopolized by the wealthy canning companies. The Americans who fished from small boats didn't like them, and the abolition of fish traps became a broadly based populist issue. In 1934, Washington voters abolished the traps by initiative. The following year, the American share of the Fraser River catch dropped to 13 per cent. All of a sudden, a guaranteed equal share looked like a pretty good deal. The state withdrew its objections, and the treaty with Canada was ratified in 1937, to take effect in 1944.

Under the terms of the treaty, passages for salmon were created around the obstruction in Hell's Gate Canyon, and the Fraser River runs soon grew larger than they had been for thirty years. Since 1946, fishermen of both nations have been regulated with minimal friction, Canadian and American biologists have kept close track of the fish runs, and spawning channels have been jointly built and maintained to make the sockeyes' life in the Fraser system a little easier.

All has gone exceedingly well by most standards, but in recent years Canadian representatives have argued that they deserve more than an equal share. (Actually, the Canadians get about 60 per cent. Not all Fraser River salmon approach the river mouth through waters included in the international agreement. Some approach it through the Johnson Strait, to the north, where only Canadians catch them.) For one thing, the Canadians say, although the United States has historically paid half the cost of restoring and preserving the Fraser River runs—and the American contribution of cash and technology looked crucial to the Canadians before World War II—the U.S. really hasn't earned 50 per cent of the fish. Canada has paid more than its share, they reason, by foregoing the building of large dams on the river, a type of sacrifice that the United States has been conspicuously unwilling to make on its own Columbia River.

They also point out that all those sockeye, as well as salmon of other species caught along the Alaskan panhandle, are spawned in Canadian streams, and that when the United States is speaking in international forums about salmon fishing by Japan, it argues strongly that—with the exception of Fraser River sockeye—salmon should belong to the nation in which they spawn.

"It's a question of Canada's sovereignty," George Hewison, secretary-treasurer of the United Fishermen and Allied Workers Union of British Columbia, has said. The United States "can totally despoil the Columbia River and then say, 'Canada, you've gotta supply all the answers.'" Hewison has pointed out that the value of fish caught in British Columbia equals the value of fish caught in all of Canada's eastern Maritime Provinces, and that salmon account for more than half the value of the British Columbian catch. What is at stake, Hewison feels, is "millions of dollars' worth of a resource that is a heritage of future generations of Canadians." But "whenever the Americans lay down a hard line, it's automatic for us to retreat."

The Americans, for their part, have traditionally pointed out that the United States is at least half responsible for the existence of enough Fraser River salmon to be worth fighting about, and that after all, a treaty is a treaty. They have also pointed out that Canadians fishing off the west coast of Vancouver Island catch many salmon spawned in the hatcheries of Washington State. *If* the Canadians were willing to leave American fish alone, the Americans might by now be willing to reconsider the division of fish from the Fraser River. Meanwhile, it is still accurate to speak, as a Congressional staff member did a few years ago, of the United States' need to argue "one way when we're sitting in Ottawa with the Canadians and another way when we're sitting in Tokyo with the Japanese."

The Canadians don't like the Americans catching salmon beyond the river mouth. The Americans don't like the Japanese catching salmon beyond the continental shelf. The irony of the situation is obvious, but American fishermen tend not to appreciate it. Indeed, they tend to be much more

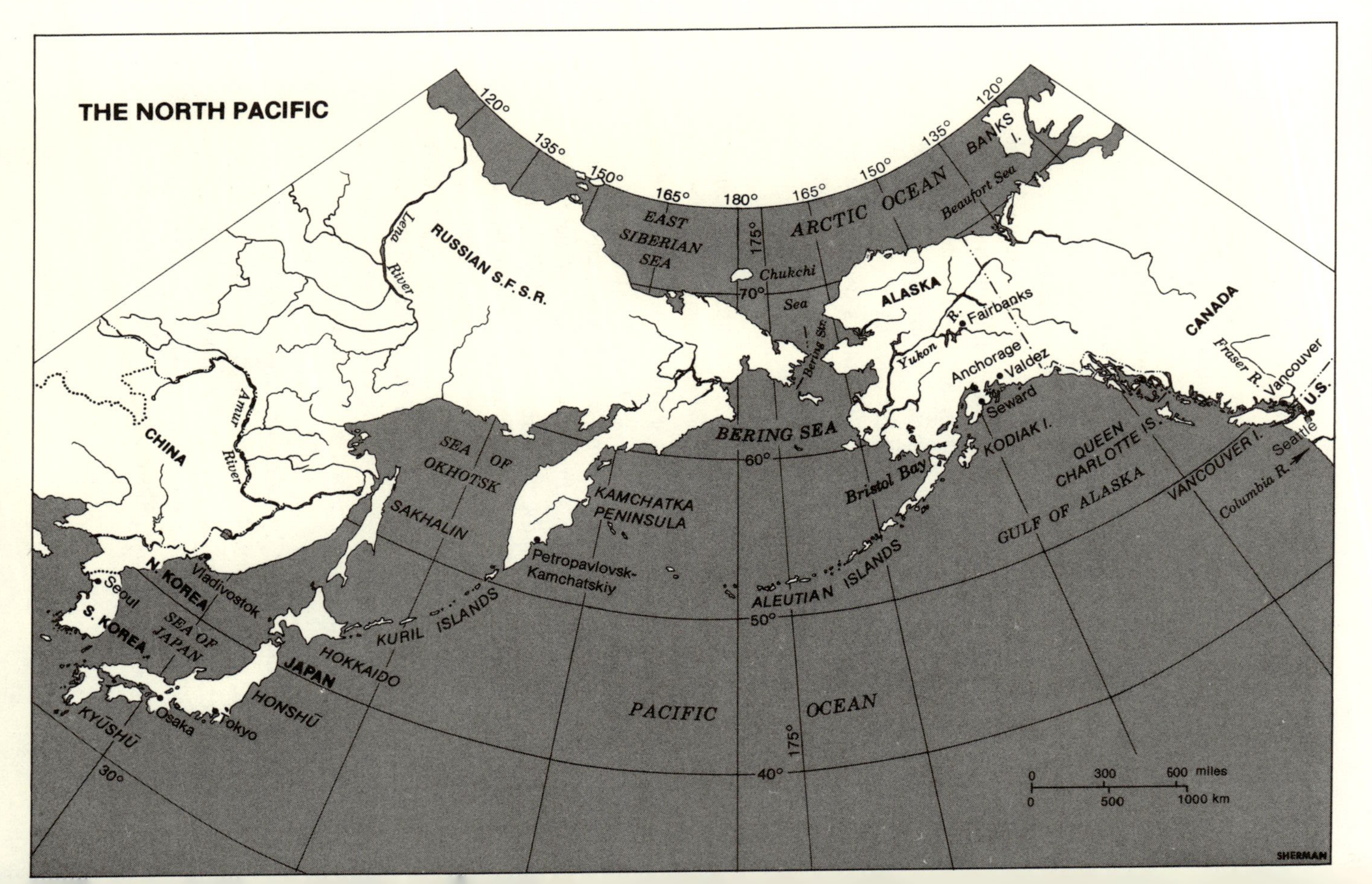

THE NORTH PACIFIC
RUSSIAN S.F.S.R.
EAST SIBERIAN SEA
ARCTIC OCEAN
Chukchi Sea
Beaufort Sea
ALASKA
Yukon
R. Fairbanks
Anchorage
Valdez
Seward
CANADA
Fraser R.
Vancouver
Seattle
U.S.
Columbia R.
BANKS I.
120°
135°
150°
165°
180°
165°
150°
135°
120°
175°
70°
Bering Str.
Bering Sea
CHINA
Amur River
Lena River
SEA OF OKHOTSK
SAKHALIN
KAMCHATKA PENINSULA
Petropavlovsk-Kamchatskiy
BERING SEA
60°
KODIAK I.
Bristol Bay
QUEEN CHARLOTTE IS.
GULF OF ALASKA
VANCOUVER I.
ALEUTIAN ISLANDS
50°
KURIL ISLANDS
HOKKAIDO
N. KOREA
Vladivostok
SEA OF JAPAN
S. KOREA
Seoul
JAPAN
HONSHŪ
Tokyo
Osaka
KYŪSHŪ
30°
PACIFIC OCEAN
40°
175°
300   500 miles
0   500   1000 km
SHERMAN

bitter than the Canadians because the conflict with Japan provides a focus for the anti-Oriental feeling that is always at least latent on the West Coast, and because there is an even stronger sense that "they" are out there where they don't belong, catching something that is "ours."

To understand what Japanese fishermen are doing out there catching Alaskan salmon, one must glance back through a long, tangled chain of historical development. Sixty years ago, they weren't out there at all. Having already wiped out most of their own salmon and having joined the worldwide scramble for markets and resources, they were fishing off Siberia, catching Russian salmon. The right to fish along the Siberian coast had been one of the spoils of Japan's victory in the Russo-Japanese War. The Japanese fished mainly along Sakhalin Island and the Kamchatka Peninsula, where the greatest number of Asiatic salmon spawn. They canned the salmon on the Siberian mainland and sold the product in Europe and Britain for foreign exchange. In the process, they broke what had been the American and Canadian monopoly of the lucrative British salmon market.

But during the 1920s, the increasingly confident Soviet government pushed the Japanese canneries out of Siberia. Unwilling to give up a profitable enterprise, the Japanese developed techniques for canning salmon aboard ship in the open sea. For several years, Japan was still permitted to fish along the Siberian coast, but by the late 1930s relations between the two countries had grown very strained and oscillated between bad and worse, depending partly on who was on better terms with Hitler at the moment.

Business Week noted in December 1936 that "Russo-Japanese tension is especially fierce just now. Moscow has suddenly turned firm on the Far Eastern fisheries question. Much of the supply comes from Soviet Far Eastern waters where the Japanese have long had the right to fish according to contracts made with the Russians. This year, Russia is

withholding those rights until Japan agrees to respect existing mutual boundaries and put an end to the ever-recurring
border clashes. It is Moscow's slapback after the German-
Japanese pact was announced." That Stalin's government
cared a great deal about fish as fish seems highly unlikely. It
seems more likely that Stalin's government found fish a use-
ful economic weapon against Japan.

A cable from Moscow in the same issue of *Business Week*
reported that, "confronted with the assertion by the Japanese
ambassador that delay in signing an extension of the
fisheries concession is causing much irritation in Japan,
Foreign Minister Litvinov promptly replied that the Japanese-
German agreement recently announced has caused even
greater irritation in Moscow."

In 1937, after Russia had grown particularly truculent,
part of the Japanese salmon fleet first appeared off the coast
of Alaska. American fishermen and canners responded in the
time-honored frontier manner: they talked of riding out with
high-powered rifles to run the trespassers off, and they sent
urgent messages to Washington. Secretary of State Cordell
Hull issued a strong warning to Japan to stay away, Japan became involved in a full-scale war with China, and the Japanese boats withdrew. But Japan said explicitly that it was not
relinquishing its right under international law to catch any
kind of fish it chose in international waters, even if those fish
happened to have been spawned in Alaskan streams.

At the end of World War II, Russia took back Sakhalin
Island and made it clear that the privilege of catching Siberian salmon was something for which Japan would have to
sweat a little, every year. It was hardly surprising, then, that
in the mid-1940s Japan turned to the open sea. American
salmon interests were eager to make sure that it didn't turn
too far. At their urging, the State Department forced Japan—
still occupied by American troops and an American military
government—to negotiate about Pacific salmon.

The negotiations took place in Tokyo in 1951 with representatives of the United States, Canada and Japan in attendance. Basically, they agreed to establish a north-south line through the Pacific Ocean, west of which the United States and Canada would abstain from catching salmon, and east of which the Japanese would abstain. Edward Allen, a Seattle attorney who was a member of the American team, has recalled the negotiations as quite amicable on all sides; but of course, he has said, the Japanese tried to have the line drawn as far east as possible, and the Americans and Canadians tried to have it drawn as far west. The result, a totally arbitrary compromise, was a line at 175 degrees west longitude, down the middle of the Pacific, well beyond Bristol Bay. The agreement was christened the International North Pacific Fisheries Treaty, and the three-nation regulatory body established to oversee it became the International North Pacific Fisheries Commission.

At the time the agreement was signed, no one knew much about what salmon did after they entered the ocean. Research would have required a lot of money and effort, and no nation had ever considered the investment worthwhile. As far as anyone knew in 1951, North American salmon did not venture beyond the continental shelf, and a legal barrier at 175 degrees west longitude would definitely protect them.

Nevertheless, the Japanese—who realized that Asian salmon could be found beyond the Asian continental shelf— went into the middle of the Pacific—staying on their side of the line—lowered their mile-long gill nets, and caught salmon, some of which were American. Meanwhile, the American catch in Bristol Bay declined. True, it had been declining for at least twenty years, but there seemed to be some connection between the fish the Japanese were catching and the fish the Americans were not. The United States began studying the ocean migration of salmon with a vengeance.

Canada and Japan did a lot of research, too—cooperative research had been one provision of the Tokyo agreement—and by 1957, they had discovered that Japanese fishermen could stay well west of 175 degrees west longitude and still catch salmon that had been spawned in Alaskan streams. It was also clear that salmon from both sides of the Pacific intermingled west of the line. The three-nation treaty said that if 175 degrees west longitude proved unsatisfactory after five years, the line could be renegotiated. In 1957, the United States began arguing that the line should be moved 10 degrees farther west.

The Japanese pointed out that fish from both continents were intermingling west of the line, so that to refrain from catching North American fish they would have to refrain from catching Asian fish, too. In short, they didn't want the line moved. After a while, they began suggesting that the line be moved 10 degrees farther east. Scientists from both the United States and Japan spent a lot of time hunting for information to support their respective countries' points of view. Edward Allen, who was involved in the negotiations, has recalled that no one ever really thought the line would be moved one way or the other; the demands and counter-demands were made for purely political reasons.

A certain amount of maneuvering has gone on ever since, with varying degrees of cordiality. In 1973, the Americans who went to Tokyo for a meeting of the International North Pacific Fisheries Commission felt that the Japanese had been insulting. In the United States, there have been congressional hearings about Pacific salmon problems, and there has been periodic talk of boycotting Japanese goods. In 1965, anticipating a banner year in Bristol Bay and being unwilling to have most of the fish intercepted at sea, American fishermen began talking to longshoremen's unions about a boycott and pressed the federal government particularly hard to ride herd on the Japanese. As a result, Japanese boats for the first time were caught fishing east of the abstention line. There have been few recorded violations since then, but Japan's observance of the treaty line has not made Japan's catching Alaskan salmon any easier for American fishermen to accept.

Late in the 1950s, the United States began calling for an end to all net fishing on the high seas. Canada, which by and large has let the United States do all the pushing for the North American side, joined in. To make their demand plausible, the two nations had to forbid the small-scale but highly lucrative net fishing that their own citizens had recently begun beyond their traditional coastal waters. Since then, the United States has generally been careful to direct its criticism toward *net* fishing. The Japanese are currently the only ones netting salmon outside coastal waters. But American trollers are out there, too, dragging hooks and lines.

The United States would presumably be willing to sacrifice its relatively small number of trollers if it could get an international ban on all high-seas fishing for salmon. What it wanted and what it would still prefer is to get the Japanese high-seas salmon fleet off the ocean altogether. Meanwhile, American fishermen and negotiators have continued to make strong cases against the biological wisdom of high-seas fishing with nets, especially as it is practiced by Japan.

For one thing, Americans argue, it is impossible for anyone fishing on the high seas to tell where any fish come from, so salmon from runs that need time to replenish themselves can't be spared. For another, salmon that are washed off nets by rough water after they have been too badly injured to survive are totally wasted, as are salmon caught by nets that have broken away and drift through the ocean trapping fish that no one will ever use. Additionally, salmon netted far out at sea are immature; they are not as heavy as they would be if they were caught later, closer to shore, so catching them in the ocean wastes a lot of potential meat. An American fisherman named Dave Hilholland has pointed out that by using nets with four-inch mesh instead of the five-and-one-eighth-inch mesh required by American regulations, the Japanese catch sockeyes that are at least a year away from maturity and are one or two pounds below their mature weight of six pounds. Another fisherman observed that he could tell "the Japs" were going after immature fish because "we catch them with scars all over their noses; we can tell they've gotten their heads into a narrow-mesh net and backed out."

All of these arguments against high-seas net fishing have merit, although in the context of the current dispute they are all somewhat beside the point. For in Japan's view, catching salmon wastefully is better than not catching them at all. And while the Japanese may not feel possessive about the salmon themselves, they certainly do feel possessive about the right to exploit the salmon. This is a feeling which the Americans who catch Fraser River salmon might be expected to recognize.

Another American argument against high-seas salmon fishing is that to preserve large salmon runs in this day and age, the nation in which they spawn must spend millions of dollars on hatcheries, fish ladders and so forth—which is actually not the case with Alaskan salmon—and must forego millions of dollars' worth of industrial development. Therefore, it is unfair for another nation to catch the salmon, and if another nation does, it is unreasonable to expect the host nation to keep spending the necessary money. "It is the host nation that bears the total cost and sacrifice necessary to perpetuate and increase the productivity of salmon streams," reads the American booklet circulated at Caracas. "There is obviously no incentive for host nations . . . to suffer such investments and sacrifices unless there are assurances that the risks of variable or reduced catch to the host nation fishermen induced by high-seas fishing by other nationals [are] substantially minimized or totally eliminated."

Such assurances may be hard to come by. International

law has always said that fish in the middle of the ocean are fair game for anyone who wants to catch them. And while it is true that salmon spawn and spend their earliest years in freshwater streams, it is also true that they do most of their eating and acquire most of their marketable meat in the "common pasture" of the unowned sea. And finally, the principle of abstention incorporated into the International North Pacific Fisheries Treaty exists no place outside that treaty and exists within it only because Japan had been defeated in war and was occupied militarily when the agreement was made. Japan will certainly not agree to abstain from fishing in the Pacific west of 175 degrees. Further abstention would be unattractive economically and repellent as an issue of sovereignty. It would also be dangerous politically, for if Japan agreed to catch fewer North American salmon, the Russians, who still drive a very hard bargain over fishing rights, might well press Japan to catch fewer Asiatic salmon, too.

The crucial fact is that Japan has invested a lot of capital in a form of fishing that has always been sanctioned by treaty and by international law, and it is unwilling to scrap that investment without substantial cause. A chance to improve the Japanese fishing companies' image as conservationists has not been cause enough. Japanese officials are aware of the dismal state of that image. They have grown quite concerned about the bad press their whaling and fishing practices have received, and they would like to put themselves in a better light. But there are limits. Akira Matsuura, the Japanese government's director of oceanic fisheries, said not long ago that he had been dismayed by the way Japan had been blamed at Caracas for the small number of salmon returning to Bristol Bay in 1974, when it had been clear—and he was correct about this—that the fish had been decimated by a very severe winter in their first year after being spawned. He also said that he hoped American fishermen did not think Japan was trying to deprive them of their livelihood. Actually, Japan wanted everyone to prosper together—"co-prosperity" was the word he used—and the good will of the Americans was important to Japan. Japanese fishermen had already been placed under "severe" restrictions for the sake of conservation, he maintained, and his country was well aware of the need to preserve "our resources and *your* resources." Japan was even willing to go further than it already had. But there was a point beyond which it could not go: the point at which its oceanic fisheries became uneconomic.

By and large, the impact of the Japanese fishing fleet on North American salmon has been relatively modest. (Much less than the effect of the Columbia River dams, for instance.) What has really worried U.S. officials for some years has been the prospect that other nations, not bound by treaty to stay west of 175 degrees west longitude, will start catching North American salmon, too. This fear is not entirely far-fetched. The South Koreans have already tried it once, and they have reserved the right to try it again.

In 1968, the South Koreans did a little exploratory fishing along the Alaskan coast, and later that year they bought a large cannery ship from Norway. They first operated their new purchase off the coast of Japan, which displeased the Japanese; then they operated it off the coast of Alaska, which displeased the Americans. In 1970, at the urging of Alaska's two senators, the Senate voted to cut off all economic aid to South Korea unless Korean fishing boats stayed out of Alaskan waters. The bill did not pass the House. The following year, Alaska's Senator Ted Stevens sponsored legislation to lop $5.8 million from a foreign aid bill that would have supplied South Korea with naval patrol boats. Stevens' bill was intended explicitly as retaliation for South Korea's catching Alaskan salmon. In detailing his case against the Koreans, Stevens said that they had "not agreed to recognize the principle of abstention that protects our salmon." The implication was that this nonrecognition made South Korea a kind of international outlaw, a unique holdout from a generally accepted international rule—which was nonsense, since the principle of abstention was unique to the International North Pacific Fisheries Treaty.

A South Korean fisheries official was subsequently quoted as saying, "We will never give up and no country can make us give up our fishing operations in the North Pacific to catch bottomfish and salmon, too. . . . The United States will walk over our dead bodies to stop us fishing for salmon in the North Pacific." American pressure and an American promise to buy more South Korean fish products persuaded the Koreans to stay out of Alaskan waters for five years, but not to renounce their right to fish anywhere outside of America's territorial limits. The Koreans are still out there in the Pacific, and American fisheries policy people are still uneasy.

Nor is South Korea the only potentially interested nation on the western Pacific rim. Taiwan has not gone after salmon, but some people think it may. In January 1975, a Taiwanese fishing boat was seen for the first time in the Bering Sea. The People's Republic of China might also choose to catch salmon, and it presumably would be harder to muscle out of the way than South Korea. And then there is Eastern Europe: the East Germans and Poles are already pursuing other species of fish in the North Pacific, and they and their neighbors are quite capable of going after salmon, too.

Such a free-for-all would leave relatively few salmon for any nation and nearly none for the small American boats, which would be last in line. Because no single nation would be likely to practice much restraint—there would be great pressure to catch the largest possible number of salmon of all ages to make the enterprise pay—it would almost certainly wipe out salmon as a major commercial resource. The salmon would probably not be eliminated in a strictly biological sense, except for the populations of certain individual streams. There would be some survivors. But the scale of many salmon runs would be greatly diminished, possibly forever. A handful of nations would have ended one of the few great free lunches of the modern world.

Ironically, the active and anticipated desire of Asian, East European and North American nations to catch Pacific salmon has nothing to do with starvation's recent progress around the world. Acquiring protein is not these countries' aim. Obviously, the big fishing nations do catch fish for domestic consumption, but not even Japan, where fish provide a larger percentage of the daily protein intake than in other industrialized nations, pursues salmon merely as a source of food. For *food* that will be accessible to the masses, the Japanese have long fished along the Northwest coast for bottomfish. (Japanese trawlers fishing along the Alaskan coast for groundfish almost wiped out the rich halibut fishery there. Although Japan claimed that catching halibut was only incidental to catching other fish, the damage was done. Before the imposition of a 200-mile limit, some fishermen feared that before long the groundfish, which the United States did not use itself, would also be seriously depleted.) If food alone were the object of salmon fishing, there would be no reason for American fishermen to fear salmon fishing by South Korea, Taiwan or mainland China. But Japan has sold canned salmon on the world market, just as the United States has, and if other nations join the fishery, they, too, will be looking for foreign exchange.

It is by no means certain, though, that they would be able to catch salmon on the high seas and sell them at a profit. As a very knowledgeable American economist has observed, "the Japanese have been losing their asses in the high-seas fishery," and economics may ultimately sink the whole enterprise. Rising labor costs have plagued the Japanese, and while they can hire cheap labor from the Asian mainland, they have no easy way around the high cost of fuel.

Viewed in terms of gallons of petroleum burned per pound of protein obtained, high-seas salmon fishing is an outrageous waste of resources, as is the constant chugging of hundreds of small salmon boats along the coasts of Washington, Alaska and British Columbia. If the price of fuel continues to rise, it may become hopelessly uneconomic to send large ships chasing relatively small numbers of fish around the North Pacific.

In the meantime, with fuel still not expensive enough to make the economics totally prohibitive, the nations involved must deal with the existing problems.

Some American fishermen were optimistic before the Caracas session that the Law of the Sea Conference would solve the problems once and for all, but that now looks unlikely. The Japanese have argued that since the Pacific salmon conflict is a unique case, it should be dealt with privately by the nations involved and not even considered by the world at large. And the world at large has had so much trouble coming to grips with more widely understood matters that even if it disagrees with Japan, it can hardly be expected to provide a quick solution.

One thing that the Caracas session did do was make it clear that, agreement or not, the 200-mile limit was an idea whose time had come. Ecuador was already enforcing it. Other nations were going to start imposing 200-mile limits unilaterally, whether or not such limits could be legally enforced. For Japan, which has long fished close to foreign coastlines in oceans around the world, this was obviously a matter of no small importance. It may well have made Japan more likely to accept the need to compromise and make deals.

By itself, a 200-mile limit will not protect North American salmon. But perhaps Japan could be persuaded to catch fewer Pacific salmon in exchange for continuing its fishing for less valuable but more numerous species closer to shore.

Or perhaps Japan could be given a guaranteed share of the mature salmon caught closer to shore if it would stop catching immature salmon on the high seas.

Whatever the formula of compromise, if one assumes that the main danger is the fishing of other East Asian and perhaps East European countries, the United States would be well advised to work out its differences with Japan. The Japanese would have to be party to any effective agreement designed to freeze those nations out and seems more than willing to do so. To gain Japan's cooperation, the United States would probably have to recognize Japan's right to a share of North American salmon—a bitter pill for some Americans to swallow but possibly the least unpleasant choice.

Yet even if the United States, Japan, Canada and Russia decided high-handedly that the North Pacific was their private lake and made an exclusionary agreement, no one is really sure it could be enforced. What if the People's Republic of China wanted to fish and were willing to make it an issue of national sovereignty? The United States has been unwilling to put really strong pressure on Japan (which has given some Northwestern fishermen a sense of having been abandoned to their fate); would it be willing to risk hostilities with China?

Economic pressures offer the only hope of a neat solution. The expectation of profit is all that could tempt new national fishing fleets to chase salmon around the North Pacific; if there is more money to be made—or less money to be lost— by staying home, then home they'll stay. If rising fuel costs make high-seas salmon fishing hopelessly unprofitable, then even the Japanese will start staying home. Some people have also speculated that Japan's high-seas salmon fleet will stay home once Japanese financial interests have penetrated the American salmon-canning industry to the point at which their stake in salmon caught by American boats exceeds their stake in Japanese-caught fish.

While the economic considerations pursue their circuitous course of evolution and the resentment of American fishermen waxes and wanes, the biological components of the salmon problem are studied more closely with each passing year. The United States, Canada, Japan, Russia, the International Pacific Salmon Fisheries Commission, the International North Pacific Fisheries Commission, the province of British Columbia, the states of Washington, Oregon and Alaska, and any number of universities have biologists studying the salmon, plotting their routes, examining their motives and keeping track of every fluctuation in their numbers. All the regulations and agreements governing salmon fishing rest on an overwhelming base of biological detail, and each international commission spends a good deal of its time discussing the latest scientific data and projections.

Our knowledge of the salmon is being extended continually, and the foundation of the ultimate international agreement, whatever that might be, is presumably being laid. And yet there is an air of futility about the entire enterprise. The essential problem is one not of knowledge but of possession.

James Crutchfield, a University of Washington economist who is co-author of *The Pacific Salmon Fisheries* and an authority on the problems of salmon in both oceans, has put it very nicely: "The idea that if you just study the fish long enough the problems will solve themselves is crazy. The real question is, 'Who gets the swag?' "

3. *Indians and Rockefellers: the Durable Cord*

EITHER the state's attorney was seriously agitated, or he was putting on a pretty good show. It was the winter of early 1974, and the Washington State Supreme Court was hearing, for the second time, a case in which attorneys for a Colville Indian named Leonard Tonasket argued that the state had no authority to tax cigarettes sold at Tonasket's store on Colville reservation land. The state had no, or at best limited, jurisdiction on Indian land, they argued; the Constitution gave Congress sole power to regulate commerce with Indian tribes, and the state had no right to interfere. The state didn't accept that argument and had, in fact, raided Tonasket's business, attached his bank account and confiscated cigarettes both in and en route to his store. The state's attorney set up maps showing the proximity of Indian reservations to white population centers in Washington and painted a dire picture of the fate that would befall neighboring white businessmen if Indians were allowed to sell things on their reservations without charging tax. "You mean," asked the chief justice, leaning forward in what seemed to be astonishment, "they could sell *liquor? Pianos?*"

"Exactly, your honor," the attorney replied.

The attorney's argument had nothing to do with the letter

of the law. The point he was making with his maps was that recognizing the Indians' special legal status and preserving the whites' economic interests were incompatible. (The court ruled that Federal law gave states taxing power on Indian reservations—a notion that the U.S. Supreme Court has rejected—but that state law permitted the Tonaskets to sell each customer two cartons of cigarettes tax-free.) The state's attorney's ideas were hardly original, and hardly unique to Washington State. They seem to crop up, in one form or another, whenever Native Americans claim that law and history have given them certain special rights of sovereignty or title. The feuding over Pacific salmon shows how an established economic interest can be seen as the equivalent of a legal right. The feuding over Native American claims to sovereignty and title shows how an established economic interest can be seen as more important than a legal right.

From the perspective of the late twentieth century, it is much more convenient to regret the way in which the Indians were strong-armed and swindled out of a continent than to recognize that some of their claims to the continent may still be valid. When white civilization found them, the tribes were sovereign entities. The federal government signed treaties with them as sovereign entities. Exactly what property rights the treaties gave the Indians is unclear in many cases, but it is perfectly clear that the law still regards Indian tribes as sovereign in many respects. The idea of Indian sovereignty is not easy for most white people to accept or even grasp. It seems wildly anachronistic. If you think of it as a special status granted to primitives, it is inappropriate to Native Americans in the late twentieth century. But if you think of it as a legal right reserved to aboriginal bargaining agents and inherited by their descendants, it begins to make sense—not, perhaps, in any absolute moral terms, but in terms of the legal system on which we all rely.

Sensible or not, when the Native Americans' unique legal

status is joined to claims of ownership, people get upset. In fact, people react to Native American sovereignty much as they respond to the sovereignty of minor foreign powers. One does not generally begrudge even the most unlikely nations their own presidents and generals, their own uniforms and currency. It is all quaint and rather amusing. But when they start suggesting that their sovereignty extends to certain oil fields or copper mines or whatever, one is no longer amused.

Closer to home, a lot of people felt things had gone too far when, for example, a small, impoverished Indian tribe asked for title to a portion of its ancestral land which happened to lie along the south rim of the Grand Canyon. In 1973, a bill was introduced in Congress for the purpose of roughly doubling the size of the Grand Canyon National Park. The land added to the Park would include an area along the Canyon rim on which the Havasupai Indians, who live on 500 acres at the bottom of Havasu Canyon, graze their horses and cattle during the summer. The land was already under federal management. The Havasupai had to get a new grazing permit every year, and they weren't allowed to erect living places there. The Indians wanted to be able to live at their summer grazing grounds and wanted to free themselves from the need to get a new permit every year. The bill gave them an opportunity to do so, and they consequently proposed adding to it language that would give them trust title to 250,000 acres of the canyon rim.

No one denied that the Havasupai had used the land during most of the past 1300 years, or suggested that they had misused it under the yearly permits. The tribe's poverty and cramped quarters at the bottom of the canyon were beyond question. But actually giving the Indians title to that piece of land struck a large and vocal portion of the environmental movement as out of the question. One simply couldn't turn part of the Grand Canyon over to any single bunch of people. Besides, what would they do with the land once they had it?

All of a sudden, some of the same environmentalists who

were forever legitimizing their own position by invoking the red man's traditional reverence for the land began arguing that the red man might put up condominiums along the edge of the canyon. In fact, they argued, the land wasn't good for much else. And if the red man had title to the land, he could do with it as he pleased. The Sierra Club led a serious lobbying effort against the Indians' request. The club's Washington representative, Brock Evans, said that giving title to the Havasupai would be a "disaster." (The Havasupai wound up with trust title to 185,000 acres, under terms that preclude most development.)

For some time now, the relationship between the Indians and the environmental movement has been full of irony. Indians asking for control of a resource often say that they were, after all, the "first conservationists" and can be counted on to manage it wisely. Environmentalists, eager to prove that they are not simply odd-ball holdouts from the march of civilization, often say that they are out of step only with the current exploitive civilization, that another civilization inhabited the continent for millennia with an attitude much like theirs. But time after time when specific conflicts arise, environmentalists and Indians wind up on opposite sides of the fence—a fact that causes some thoughtful environmentalists a good deal of discomfort. The root of the problem is that while environmentalists are usually trying to restrict or eliminate the economic uses of a particular area, the Indians are usually asserting ownership—which implies, by any conventional standards, the right to do as they please with it. They may choose not to exploit a resource—as the Northern Cheyenne have currently chosen to do with their immense deposit of low-sulphur coal in Montana—or they may choose to exploit it to the hilt—as the Navajo have done with the coal of Black Mesa. Either way, the choice is all theirs, which is something the environmental movement can't logically accept.

Of course, organized environmentalists aren't the only

whites who are troubled by claims of Native American ownership. The objects of those claims are seldom small and are sometimes staggering. Perhaps the most impressive assertions of Native American ownership were the Eskimos', Indians' and Aleuts' successful demand for 40 million acres of Alaska and their largely successful demand for a billion dollars as payment for the rest of the state. No one questioned the fact that the natives had lived there since time immemorial and that, until recently, no one else would have willingly been caught dead on most of the land. Still, white Alaskans were outraged when the native leaders began pressing their claims in the late 1960s. "Just because somebody's grandfather chased a moose across the land doesn't mean he owns it," said Governor Hickel. That was the prevailing sentiment. Most of the state was no longer exclusively native country. The natives' own range had contracted. White people hunted over much of the state. The state government itself was eager to select land that was rich in petroleum and other minerals. What did the natives think they were doing?

Ownership of land in the European sense had never been a part of native culture, but that didn't mean that either the older and more traditional or the younger, college-educated natives were free of possessive feelings about the land. In 1970, Emil Notti, then president of the Alaska Federation of Natives, said, "I fly into villages and sit down with the village men to talk. I tell them that the state can take their land and . . . can sell it or do whatever it wants. They get angry. They say, 'My father had a camp here and my grandfather had a camp twenty-five miles over there. I inherited the land from them, and I want to pass it down to my children.' " Certainly the various native groups had fought fiercely with each other in defense of what each considered its land.

At a 1969 Congressional hearing, John Borbridge, then head of the Tlingits' and Haidas' organization, was asked, "When the Russians took possession of the area which they occupied, was there resistance to their occupancy and was there intent to exclude them from the place?"

Borbridge replied, "Mr. Congressman, I am very pleased that you asked that question. In Yakutat the Russians were—there may be a politer word than 'massacre' but we drove them out. . . . When the Russians wanted fish or when they wanted game they recognized that this was the land of the Tlingits and Haidas so that we in effect were establishing our dominion as of that time and this was clearly recognized by them."

The native leaders—who carried on the land claims fight largely without the knowledge of many of their constituents in the remote villages—were convinced that they had a sound legal claim to the land. No one had ever bought or taken it from them, so it was still theirs. They were also convinced that if they didn't proceed as if they had a sound claim, they would wind up with very little. An Athabascan leader named Alfred Ketzler explained in a letter to *The New Republic* that "to those who view [the land claims] issue as one of alleviating poverty and not involving property rights, our demand for some $10,000 and 800 acres per capita seems unreasonable and even outrageous." A recognition of the property rights involved "is the keystone to a fair, generous and just settlement of our land claims." In a more philosophical vein, Frederick Paul, then the attorney for the Arctic Slope Native Association, wrote, "Why is it that if the [state] wants to build a road over a white man's property, automatically one knows the [state] must pay him its fair value; but when the [state] wants Indian lands, one worries about the need of the Indians and justifies payment and the amount thereof by the criterion of need? . . .

"Why is it . . . that the amount of payment must be excused by 'what is necessary for the future economic and social development of the community,' as Walter J. Hickel, then governor, suggested? . . .

"How about the white man's rule of fair value?"

The natives never did manage to convince a lot of influential whites—not even some of their best friends, as it were—that their case would stand up in court. They made it quite plain, though, that they wouldn't hesitate to go to court and tie up North Slope oil development indefinitely unless their claims were settled generously. Their occupancy of the land and the plausibility of their legal arguments put them in a position to do so. Congress gave them most of what they asked.

Some of the natives' main opposition in Congress had come from both conservative and liberal politicians who represented other states with large Indian populations. In Alaska, it was possible to give the natives a lot without really taking from anyone else; in the more populous and more developed states of the "lower 48," it was not. And if the Alaskan natives got away with this, who knew what the Indians back home would try asking for? It was not a matter of questioning the legal or historical validity of the Alaskan natives' claims but of protecting the economic and political status quo.

Outside Alaska—and Maine, if the Penobscot and Passamaquoddy Indians had not scaled down their claim to two-thirds of the state—the assertion of Native American rights probably poses the greatest potential threat to the status quo in the arid regions of the West. There, the scant supply of water has long been the object of intense competition among white farmers, industrialists and population centers. Indians have not added much to the demand. But the Winters Doctrine, created by a 1908 ruling of the United States Supreme Court, gives Indian tribes a right to virtually any water that flows through or by their reservations. The Court reasoned that the government established reservations in order to turn the Indians into settled agriculturalists. They couldn't practice agriculture without water, so a right to use water was implied by the establishment of the reservations. The Court did not suggest any limit to that right, and more recent Court decisions have reaffirmed it. The Court's 1976 decision in the Cappaert case seems to extend the Winters Doctrine to underground water supplies.

Until the mid-1970s, the doctrine remained rather obscure. It is no longer obscure, though, and there can hardly be a tribal lawyer anywhere in the arid West who is entirely ignorant of it or its potential. In water-short Arizona, some tribes have already begun invoking the Winters Doctrine.

It is not as if they had just discovered the value of water. Many Arizona Indians irrigated for centuries. In many cases, white society gained access to the water by shoving Indians out of the way. A historical report delivered to the Gila River Indian Community in 1974 by Nicklason Associates of Washington, D.C., observed that, "For several centuries prior to the mid-1800s, the Gila River Pima and Maricopa Indians lived as farmers irrigating their lands in northern Mexico. [The area didn't become part of the United States until 1853.] Under their care the luxuriant bottom land of the Gila River Valley produced crops plentiful for their needs and the needs too, after the 1853 Gadsden Purchase, of white emigrants and military troops on the Overland Trail. Beyond the provision of food to these groups the Pimas and Maricopas also provided a safe haven against other, hostile Indian tribes whose marauding life style would have otherwise made hazardous the entire Gila Valley.

"A hard irony arose from that fact. Because of the safety the tribes provided them, white settlers as early as the late 1860s moved onto the land above the Indians on the river and, in the process of their irrigation, diverted the water of the Gila River to the detriment of the tribes below. As the settlers still later increased in number, as far as 100 to 150 miles upstream, the Pimas and Maricopas at first gave up their second, summer crop and eventually their single remaining crop until by 1900, because of the lack of irrigating water, their once-lush valley turned into a desolated land grown up in weeds."

Farther south around Tucson, where the Papago Indians now live in a desert, nineteenth-century maps show swampland, and surviving correspondence shows that the Indians once asked the government to give them a sawmill so that they could take advantage of the huge mesquite trees that grew there. Now, the Papagos are suing everyone around, including the mines, the City of Tucson and a huge pecan orchard, for the rights to the underground water. The Indians don't really want to deprive white society of all its water, but they do want white society to listen to them and have found that litigation is a great attention-getter.

And they do have an extremely promising legal case. If it turns out that the Indians in Arizona or anyplace else in the arid West really own most of the water, the economic impact and the resulting bitterness will be immense.

At this point, however, the assertion of Native American rights has probably had its greatest economic impact and aroused the most bitterness, not in the arid regions, but in the rainy western portion of Washington State. There, despite the Tonaskets and various other Indians who have disturbed the state government by selling cigarettes and fireworks tax-free, the main conflict has concerned Indian sovereignty over, not land, but fish.

When Governor Isaac Stevens signed a series of treaties with the Indians of western Washington in 1854 and 1855 to acquire their land for the United States, the main thing they wanted to retain, evidently, was the right to continue fishing. As U.S. District Court Judge George Boldt observed in a historic 1974 decision, "One common cultural characteristic among all of these Indians was the almost universal and generally paramount dependence upon the products of an aquatic economy, especially anadromous fish [which include salmon and steelhead trout]. . . . At the treaty negotiations, a primary concern of the Indians whose way of life was so heavily dependent upon harvesting anadromous fish was that they have freedom to move about to gather food, particularly salmon . . . at their usual and accustomed fishing places. . . . Reluctant to be confined to small reservation bases, the Indian negotiators insisted that their people continue to fish as they had beyond the reservation boundaries. There is no indication that the Indians intended or understood the language [of the treaties] . . . to limit their right to fish in any way."

It was not long before the Indians began getting elbowed out of their historical fishing spots. Sometimes the elbow was a legal one—the Nisqually Indians had the Nisqually River gerrymandered entirely out of their reservation by act of Congress in 1906—but usually it received legal sanction after the fact or not at all. In 1899, the secretary of the Smithsonian Institution, Richard Rathbun, wrote in a chronicle of salmon fishing at Point Roberts, Washington, "The principal reef-net ground of the entire region lies directly off its southeast corner, a large, kelp-covered ledge, to which the Indians have undoubtedly resorted for many generations, and which has been the cause of much contention among the several neighboring tribes. The perpetual right to fish upon it, in common with other inhabitants of the territory, was secured to the Indians by treaty with the United States in 1855, and while formerly regarded solely in the light of a rich collecting-ground where their own needs could be readily met, it afterwards became the source of much revenue in their dealings with the whites. . . . In recent years their number has varied from 150 to 200, though sometimes reaching 250. Their canoes in active operation have been as many as 15 to 20, but lately the number has greatly fallen off through the intervention of the whites. Their drying racks formerly covered a considerable area, but they are now small in extent and have been entirely driven from Cannery Point, their principal location in more prosperous days. After the completion in 1894 of the continuous line of [white-owned fish] traps commanding the approaches to the big reef, its value for reef-net fishing seems to have been in great part destroyed, and the Indian catches declined so much in consequence as to render the old-time occupation practically unprofitable. The primitive methods are making way for those of civilization, and the process has not been wholly devoid of certain elements of injustice."

By and large, Indians were not harassed for fishing on their reservations. (A 1934 edition of *The Seattle Times* did carry a story about an Indian tribe on the Olympic Peninsula that had to call in surveyors to prove that one of its members, arrested for illegal fishing on public land, had actually been 400 feet inside the reservation at the time.) But the reservations were generally small and not necessarily in the best fishing spots. Off the reservations, catching salmon in the rivers with nets was prohibited by white fishing regulations, and Indians were not thought to have any right that transcended those regulations. After a while, few Indians tried fishing outside their reservations unless they owned or worked on commercial boats. A few kept it up, though, and in the early 1960s, when the civil-rights movement brought ethnic militancy into vogue, a few started fishing as a political act, to assert what they claimed were their treaty rights.

The "fish-in" movement began on the Puyallup and Nisqually Rivers, led originally by a burly Indian named Robert Satiacum. It received national attention for a while when Marlon Brando and Dick Gregory joined the fishermen, and Gregory was arrested.

The essential question being tested by the fish-ins was whether or not Indians fishing off reservations had any right to take fish in places, at times or with equipment forbidden to white citizens. The treaties said only that Indians would retain the right to fish at their "usual and accustomed" places, "in common with the citizens of the territory." What did "in common with" mean? State fish and game officials and their white constituents argued that it gave Indians exactly the same rights as everyone else. The relative handful of militant Indians and their attorneys argued that it meant only that white citizens couldn't be totally excluded. Indians and white allies were getting arrested right and left, so they had ample opportunity to make this argument in court.

Unfortunately for both sides in the dispute, the early court decisions settled virtually nothing. The first step toward a settlement was the United States Supreme Court's 1968 decision in the *Puyallup* case. No one was terribly happy with the *Puyallup* decision. The Indian side was unhappy because the Court said the state did have a right to regulate Indian fishing off reservations. The state was unhappy because the Court said it had a right to regulate off-reservation fishing only if such regulation was necessary for conservation of the fish, and the state hadn't proven that necessity. The Indians' basic rights under the treaties remained totally unclear. Indians kept fishing. State officials kept arresting and abusing them.

The next step toward defining the treaty rights was taken by U.S. District Court Judge Robert Belloni in a 1969 case brought by Yakima Indian fishermen on the Columbia River. Belloni ruled that—as Indian attorneys had been arguing for some time—the chief purpose of state "conservation" laws was to divvy up the salmon among competing groups of white commercial and sports fishermen. The laws did not set aside a share for the Indians, but the laws had better start doing so. "There is no reason to believe," Belloni said, "that a ruling which grants the Indians their full treaty rights will affect the necessary escapement of fish in the least. The only effect will be that some of the fish now taken by sportsmen and commercial fishermen must be shared with the treaty

Indians, as our forefathers promised over a hundred years ago." Belloni was not saying that the Indians deserved the fish in return for wrongs done their ancestors. He was saying they had a right to the fish because of legally binding documents their ancestors signed.

Belloni didn't define the right beyond an "equitable" share of the fish, and anyway, his ruling didn't apply to the streams of western Washington, where the conflict was most bitter and violent. There, Indians kept fishing, and state officials kept running them in, often confiscating their boats and gear and sometimes roughing them up. There were documented cases of state game wardens attacking Indian men, women and children with tear gas, blackjacks and six-celled flashlights.

The conflict dragged on and on with nobody entirely sure of what the legalities would ultimately turn out to be. Finally, in an attempt to settle things once and for all, the United States Attorney's office for western Washington filed suit on behalf of the Indians against the state. The purpose of the suit, which was known as *U.S. v. Washington*, was to bring out all the evidence and let the courts really decide what the treaties meant. The government was joined, *amicus curiae*, by a number of the tribes. While the suit was pending, the state by and large refrained from arresting Indian fishermen with its former zeal; until the suit was settled, state officials figured, no judge was going to convict anyone anyway.

The case was tried before U.S. District Judge George Boldt, whose decision, issued in February 1974, was a bombshell. Boldt had taken the case very seriously. He left certain details for a second trial, and concentrated solely on the meaning of the treaties. Even so, his decision filled 254 pages. Interested attorneys felt that Boldt had tried hard to make sure that his decision would not be reversed. It was clearly designed to establish *all* the relevant facts, and it emerged as a massive compendium of history, anthropology and jurisprudence.

What he concluded was that the Indians had a legal right to half the fish. The treaties hadn't *given* them that right; the treaties had *reserved* to them a right they already had. As for the language of the treaties, Boldt went back to mid-nineteenth-century sources and asserted that "by dictionary definition and as intended and used in the Indian treaties and in this decision, 'in common with' means *sharing equally* the opportunity to take fish at 'usual and accustomed grounds and stations.' "

To say that white fishermen had a hard time accepting this decision would be an understatement. Here were people whose families had been fishing for two and three generations being told that someone else had a prior right to half the fish. (Actually, Boldt had said that the Indians had a right to take *up to* half the fish that could be caught at or on the way to one of their traditional fishing places without endangering the survival of a particular fish run. If the Indians lacked the equipment or manpower to catch half the fish, white fishermen didn't have to let the rest go by.) Their economic welfare seemed endangered, and so did their way of life. They had a hard time believing that Boldt had been led by logic alone to conclusions which struck them as so menacing and so unjust. Some of them sought other explanations. Had Boldt been bought off? One of the more fanciful theories was that Weyerhaeuser and other big corporations interested in commercial "fish farming" wanted all the competition out of the way; they knew they couldn't buy off the yeoman white fishermen, so they bought off the judge and in due time they would also buy off the more-easily-corrupted Indians, thereby securing a monopoly of the salmon industry. (This theory remained in circulation for more than three years.) Even without such fanciful rationales, many people believed that Boldt's decision would be thrown out entirely on appeal. That they should have wanted to believe such a thing was perfectly natural. That they should have been allowed to believe it suggests that whoever was supposed to be giving them informed counsel failed miserably. The cause of this failure may have been political expedience or it may have been sheer incompetence. Where the state government was concerned, it seems to have been the latter. Evidently, the state's legal officers never believed personally in Indian sovereignty or Indian rights, and their professional advice was that Indian sovereignty and Indian rights didn't exist. Almost three years after Boldt's decision, Washington's assistant attorney general in charge of fisheries told a group of irate fishermen that the decision was "morally reprehensible and unconstitutional." With legal advice like that, it is hardly surprising that people were shocked in 1975 when the Ninth U.S. Circuit Court upheld Boldt's decision unanimously.

The decisions did not end the problem. The Indians did not consider themselves entirely free from harassment and were still not granted any special rights to the Fraser River salmon, which were covered by an international agreement between the United States and Canada and had not been included in Boldt's decision. The state, faced with a division of salmon between the whites and more than two dozen separate tribes, caught between Boldt's decision and the decisions of county judges, felt that it was faced with a totally unmanageable situation, one in which the salmon could not be adequately protected. And the white fishermen were still not resigned to their fate. The commercial fishermen still felt that their livelihoods were being taken from them. And the sports fishermen, as a congressional staff member observed, were "in some cases more emotional than the commercial fishermen about 'their' fish." Being more numerous as well, the sports fishermen exerted a greater influence on many local politicians.

Among the commercial fishermen, many of the same people who feel that the federal government's agreement with

Canada gives them an absolute, perfectly legitimate right to catch Fraser River salmon have never accepted the idea that the same government's agreements with the Indian tribes give Indians comparable rights to catch salmon spawned in western Washington. Ironically, both the treaty with Canada and the treaties with the tribes—as defined by Boldt—confer exactly the same thing: the right to "share equally" in the fish. The Canadian agreement is a lot more recent, and its language is a lot more precise. The Indian treaties have required interpretation, and an interpretation—even if it has won the approval of higher-court judges who are far removed from its impact—is easy to reject. Since Boldt announced his interpretation of the treaties, there have been white "fish-ins," muttering about going out with shotguns to defend one's livelihood, harassment of state fishery officials, rammings, widespread poaching, some shots actually fired and a general residue of resentment.

One third-generation fisherman said within the space of a single brief conversation, "I have a lot of Indian friends" and "I *hate* Indians." Why should Indians—represented in many white minds by the Indians one saw reeling drunkenly through the seedier downtown parts of Washington cities— enjoy some special right to the fish? As one fisherman argued, "I don't expect anyone to give me anything special because I'm Yugoslavian."

An attorney for Indians in the Northwest has explained the feeling of such whites as the same kind of resentment people waiting outside a theater feel toward the guy who cuts in at the front of the line.

As the early Indians were shoved out of the way, white people moved into the spaces they vacated. If the Indians are to move back, they must now shove someone else out of the way. The injustice is then compounded. The easiest way to find one's path through this moral labyrinth is by ignoring the question of whether or not a group of contemporary red men *deserve* some valuable right as reparation for wrongs done to ancestors they never knew, abandoning morality *per se,* and following the coarse but durable cord of ownership. That is the approach that white society takes toward its own members. No one asks whether or not the Rockefellers deserve their millions, just whether or not the law allows the Rockefellers to possess them.

If one takes that same simple, amoral approach toward Native American claims, however, one still encounters the familiar conflicts between what is right and what is practical. One has simply replaced morality with the letter of the law, and neither is economically convenient. The economic system has no trouble coping with the Rockefellers' ownership of their millions; in fact, there are those who argue that the economic system has been set up so people like the Rockefellers can own millions. But the system has not been set up to accommodate the possibility that the Pimas and Papagos and other Arizona Indians control most of the water in their arid state; that the Havasupai own part of the Grand Canyon; that the Eskimos, Indians and Aleuts own 400 millon acres of Alaska; that the Penobscots and Passamaquoddies own most of Maine; or that the Muckleshoots, Nisquallies and other treaty tribes have a right to half the fish in western Washington. When such possibilities arise, many people feel threatened and are genuinely shocked. Often, their shock turns into lingering resentment. It just doesn't seem right that certain kinds of people should own certain things. Beyond the substantive issues of geopolitics, petrodollars and the rest, people were just downright offended to discover that the Arabs—still largely camel drivers in the public mind—actually owned all that oil. And far beyond any questions of legality, people have been just downright offended to discover that the Indians actually own all that land or water, or all those fish. The question is, how far beyond issues of legality does society want to go? At what point and for whose benefit should inconvenient laws and treaties be ignored or discarded? Is justice supposed to be truly blind? If it is, then what is sauce for the Rockefellers must presumably be sauce for the Muckleshoots, too.

4. Harnessing a River

In the early 1940s, soon after the Grand Coulee Dam had risen 355 feet above the natural level of the Columbia River, filling the gap between two high basalt cliffs, the folksinger Woody Guthrie wrote a song that called it "the biggest thing built by the hand of a man," and said it would "run the great factories and water the land." There was a lot of industrial romanticism in Guthrie's song, and the sentiment may sound rather naive today, but there was idealism about dam-building at that time, and within a few years there was genuine idealism about the development of nuclear reactors, too. Harnessing the river, harnessing the atom, harnessing anything that will reduce the strain and drudgery of human labor or increase its productivity will look attractive in a society in which most people are still in touch with physical labor or a need to produce. To begin with, a new source of power will inevitably seem infinite. One will be conscious of its amplitude, not its limits, and certainly not the competition for access to it which those limits imply.

Grand Coulee harnessed a lot of power. At the time it was built, it was the largest single producer of electricity in the world. The series of dams of which it is part is still the world's greatest single hydroelectric system.

A great deal was gained when the dams were built, and some things were lost. One of the losses was aesthetic. A dam has its own aesthetic, and Grand Coulee glowing in the late afternoon sun is a sight not easily forgotten, but the construction of the Columbia River dams has turned most of the river—which moves a greater volume of water than any other American river except the Mississippi—into a long lake. The conflict between the production of power and the aesthetic attractions of a free-flowing river is hardly new. It wasn't new even when Guthrie wrote that song. Back in 1902, the choice was between running the Niagara River through turbines or letting it spill freely over Niagara Falls. As Mark Sullivan recalled twenty-four years later in *Our Times,* "Agitation about diverting water from Niagara Falls for industrial purposes arrayed the public in two groups, one favoring increased use of the Falls for electrical power, the other advocating limitation, with the object of preserving the Falls in their natural beauty." The debate ended with the United States and Canada agreeing to limit the amount of water that could be diverted for industrial purposes. No one agreed to practice such restraint on the Columbia, and by now all but one of the major potential dam sites has been filled.

Perhaps more significant than the trading of kilowatts for free-flowing water has been the trading of kilowatts for salmon. When Lewis and Clark discovered the Columbia and for decades afterward, it was the world's greatest salmon river. Clark wrote that "the multitude of this fish is almost inconceivable." As early as 1872, the salmon canning business along the river brought in more than $2 million a year. The building of the dams along the Columbia declared that the river's most important product was no longer fish but electricity. It is true that fish ladders have been built at the dams downstream from Grand Coulee (which is itself too high) and that the annual salmon catch still amounts to millions of pounds. It is also true that the total reported catch in 1970 was only about a third of the 1880 figure. The main event on the Columbia is no longer the final journey of big, dying fish homeward bound from the sea, but the sheer, plunging motion of the water itself, surging through the huge, sinking pipes, swirling around the generators, foaming out into the river below, having imparted some of its own motion to the uncountable billions of electrons coursing out through the wires.

In an industrial society, the trading of fish for energy seems inevitable. That kind of trade can be found almost everywhere. Along the mill streams of early-nineteenth-century New England, fish were traded for the unadorned power of falling water; the building of mill dams kept the salmon from reaching their spawning grounds and was at least partly responsible for transforming the New England salmon from a staple food into a biological rarity. In this century, on the Columbia and elsewhere, fish have been traded for electricity. They may very well be traded for petroleum as oil drilling expands in the rich waters off the Alaskan coast and big tankers carry oil south through the waters of southeastern Alaska, British Columbia and Puget Sound. (An unsuccessful and quickly forgotten suit against the construction of the Trans Alaska Pipeline was brought by the fishermen's union of tiny Cordova, Alaska, near the pipeline's southern terminus of Valdez. The Cordova fishermen were afraid that one big oil spill or a steady accrual of small ones would destroy their sole source of livelihood.) Similarly, all over the United States prime farm land is traded daily for factory sites and shopping centers and parking lots. Prime timber-producing land is traded for real estate developments.

Presumably, these trades represent an evolutionary process. The process may well be inevitable (one tends to think that way about evolution) and irreversible (one doesn't expect to bulldoze the shopping center to bring back the cabbage patch). It may be a localized example of society's evolution from a hunting or agricultural stage to industrialism. It may reflect the evolution of human technology toward greater complexity. It may in fact be many different things to many different people. But one aspect of its character is absolutely clear: it does not involve only man, his environment and his machines. It also involves money. This is not a barter economy, and if one economic use of a resource replaces another, the reason is generally that the second use creates more wealth than the first. Often, the use that creates more wealth requires a greater initial investment. In every one of the trades mentioned above—fish for energy, farms for shopping centers, and so on—that use more dependent on money (more capital-intensive) prevails.

As that happens, old economic conflicts may be translated into new terms. On the Columbia, the supply of salmon once seemed virtually limitless. Even later observers than William Clark believed that there were enough salmon for everyone. A later nineteenth-century visitor wrote in *Harper's New Monthly* that although "in this year, 1873, more than two millions of pounds [of salmon] were put up in tin cans on the lower Columbia alone, besides fifteen or twenty thousand barrels of salted salmon," he had been "assured by the fishermen that the salmon do not decrease in numbers or in size." But before the end of the century, it became clear that if everyone were allowed to catch all the fish he wanted by any means he chose, the Columbia River salmon were doomed. The states of Oregon and Washington consequently started to regulate fishing times and methods. The state regulations have grown tighter and more complex over the years, but the underlying principle has stayed the same: the salmon should be divided among the greatest possible number of taxpayers and voters. The only widely used method of catching salmon that has ever been ruled out of order is the trap (including a special Columbia River variation called the fish wheel). Traps were expensive to build, but they were also the most efficient, economically rational means of catching salmon. Their efficiency—and the fact that they were available only to people with a lot of capital—is exactly what caused their downfall. They were banned because instead of spreading the salmon around as widely as possible, they concentrated the catch in relatively few wealthy hands.

Replacing many of the salmon with kilowatts has not eliminated the question of whether or not a large share of the resource will be funneled into relatively few hands. When the first dams went up, the control of electricity was an important national issue. As electric power gained a bigger and bigger place in American life, people began arguing about who should control access to it. Should private industry monopolize the generating facilities? Should private industry monopolize the distribution systems?

During the first third of the century, Progressives fought hard for public power, and conservatives fought hard against it. The battle intensified during the 1920s and early 1930s.

Construction of the Columbia River dams marked a decisive stage in that battle. Ever since World War I, Congress had been arguing over the operation of the Muscle Shoals power plant, which the federal government had begun building on the Tennessee River during the War. Was it good sense for the government to operate such a plant, or was it socialism? (The two were seldom equated, as they are seldom publicly equated today.) Congress passed two bills that would have approved the federal operation of Muscle Shoals, but Republican presidents vetoed them, and the conflict was not resolved until Franklin D. Roosevelt's administration. Then, the government committed itself, not only to the operation of a single plant, but to the building and operation of all the power dams in the Tennessee Valley Authority. In the Northwest, the government committed itself to the building and operation of power dams on the Columbia River. The Bonneville Project Act, passed to govern distribution of power from the dams, gave preference to cooperatives—which, with federal financing, were bringing electricity to the rural areas—and to publicly-owned utilities.

The right of the government to build and operate dams has not survived as a burning issue. But the question of who gets to use the power from the dams has not gone away. Publicly-generated power is not spread randomly among the public. Currently, some 40 per cent of the electricity for which the Columbia's salmon have been traded flows to private industry for the production of aluminum. The electricity flows, in other words, to the concentration of capital. It does so for several reasons. Aluminum is separated from its oxide by an electrolytic process, the purified metal collecting on the charged carbon linings of large "pots." This process is essentially the one that was invented independently by an American, Charles Martin Hall, and a Frenchman, Paul L.T. Heroult, in 1886. The timing of Hall's and Heroult's invention was not random. Aluminum was first isolated in 1825 by the Danish scientist Hans Christian Oersted. But not much of it could be produced until large amounts of electricity became available in the mid-1880s. Britain had a commercial generating plant in 1881. Thomas A. Edison threw the switch on the first commercial generating plant in the United States in 1882. Four years later, the world had a technique for producing aluminum in quantity.

The production of aluminum still requires more electricity than any other common, large-scale industrial operation—up to eight kilowatt-hours of electricity to produce one pound of metal. The aluminum industry therefore gravitates to places in which electricity is plentiful and cheap. Roughly one-third of the aluminum produced in the United States comes from the Northwest. The region is far from commercial sources of bauxite, the basic ore, and far from most major markets. But it is well supplied with cheap electricity, much of it from the Columbia River dams.

Inevitably, the industry's voracious appetite for energy has drawn a lot of criticism. Critics have argued, in effect, that the industry converts kilowatts into beer cans—which is true but not the whole truth. The industry also ultimately converts kilowatts into aircraft, rail transit cars, automobile parts, electrical wiring, home siding and other products of genuine social utility. The critics argue that Congress never intended the industry to capture such a large share of the Columbia's power—which would seem to be true, since the relevant federal legislation gives priority to publicly-owned distribution systems. And they say that by exporting aluminum ingots in which cheap electricity is a basic raw material, the industry is actually exporting energy needed at home.

In 1975, Congressman Jim Weaver of Oregon observed that Northwestern aluminum companies had recently exported some two hundred million pounds of ingots. "It takes 1400 million kilowatt hours of electricity to produce the 200 million pounds of ingots," Weaver said. "That is equal to all of the electricity consumed in Eugene in one year. Translated into oil, it means we're exporting [the] equivalent of 842,000 barrels."

Weaver also noted that if the contracts then being considered by the Bonneville Power Administration (BPA) went into effect, the industry would be getting its energy for the equivalent of five cents a barrel.

It requires little imagination to understand why the aluminum industry wants to be in the Northwest. Why the Northwest and the BPA have welcomed the aluminum industry is less obvious.

Aluminum refining doesn't produce many jobs per megawatt—it requires 1827 megawatt-hours to create one job for one year, compared to 146 for making steel. Still, as the industry observes, it does produce jobs. And one can't totally separate the production of aluminum from the high-employment industries, such as aircraft manufacturing, which require the metal.

A report prepared for the Western Aluminum Producers in 1974 by Arthur D. Little stated that "the aluminum industry in the Northwest employed 10,900 persons directly in 1972, which in turn supported 28,200 jobs in nonbasic industries in the region. . . . Local and state taxes paid by the aluminum industry exceeded $14.4 million." However high the price in kilowatts, many politicians have always been eager to get and retain the jobs and taxes that aluminum manufacturing provides.

The regional desire for jobs and tax revenue is easy enough to comprehend. What seems stranger, at first glance, is that the industry was originally welcomed as a consumer, as well as a provider—as a consumer of electricity. For many years after World War II, the regional market couldn't absorb the full generating capacity of the dams that had been and were being built along the Columbia. Selling power was the way in which the federal government was going to pay off the capital cost of building the dams. The more it could sell, the more quickly that capital cost could be paid off. A surplus of power was the last thing it wanted. The aluminum industry helped to avoid surplus.

The localized fear of surplus has been a consistent part of energy planning, not only in the Northwest. The builders of a big thermal generating plant, for example, will line up blue-chip industrial customers well in advance of construction, so a market for the power is assured and bonds to finance construction can be sold.

Despite the illusion of unleashing infinite power that may accompany the building of a Grand Coulee, the production of energy, like the catching of fish, is an economic process. One does not simply produce energy. One produces energy in metered units, assigns them a certain cost and sells them at a certain price.

Just as one can't understand the competition for fish unless one thinks of the fish as commodities with a certain commercial value, one can't understand the production of energy unless one thinks of kilowatts or BTUs in the same way.

Whether one is building a power plant or extracting resources from the ground, one is dealing ultimately in commodities. One does not want to produce more than one can sell, and one does not want to drive prices down. If the price seems too low, one won't even bother to produce. Pricing, therefore, determines how much oil, coal or uranium is extracted at any given time. Pricing as much as geology determines how much will be extracted in the future. A 1974 article in *The New York Times Magazine* quoted a young Texas oilman as saying, "This fella wants me to go in with him on opening up 116 shut-down wells. At $3.25 a barrel, I wouldn't even think of it. Now, with oil up at a decent price, why I just might—I'm going to talk to him tomorrow. You know, independent operators, people who think the way I think—we find 80 per cent of the oil in this country." The 1975 annual report of the Federal Resources Corporation noted that "the dramatic turn-around in the price for uranium (from $6.00 to $23.00 per pound in two years) assures a bright future [for the company's uranium properties, and] . . . more than vindicates our postponement of production at these properties." There is reason to believe that a similar logic kept the major oil companies from "discovering" the North Slope oil fields for years: the companies feared that a flood of cheaply produced Alaskan oil would depress the price of oil produced elsewhere in the United States. In one of the first major articles about the North Slope discovery, at the beginning of 1969, *Business Week* observed that "oil producers are sweating over the possibility that when cheap Arctic oil begins invading the market in 1971 or 1972 [The long delays in building the Trans Alaska Pipeline were not then foreseen.] the present price structure . . . may crack. . . . No one—certainly not the major oil companies that will determine the pace of Alaskan oil development—wants a repetition of what happened after the East Texas find of the 1930s," when prices plummeted.

Even sunlight, for all its ubiquity, will find a place in the economy only if prices permit it to do so. In fact, if one tries to chart the future of solar energy, one must talk primarily not about technology but about capital. There are many proven technologies for harnessing sunlight. There is absolutely no question that houses and household water can be heated with sunlight, or that in most parts of the United States, over a period of years, solar heating systems will cost homeowners less money than conventional systems. The problem is that a solar heating system requires a larger capital investment. Because the building costs more, the mortgage is larger, the insurance rates are higher, and so on. A solar system will therefore not be attractive to large numbers of people unless the cost of conventional systems becomes much higher, or unless either the government or private lending institutions provide a financial incentive for making the original investment.

The use of sunlight for generating electricity is even more severely restricted by a need for capital. There are many things that people do not know about the use of sunlight to generate electricity on a large scale. One thing they do know is that at this point, the capital cost of a solar generating system would dwarf the capital cost of any conventional system.

From now on, building any new central-station generating plant, solar or not, will be very expensive, and the necessary capital won't be easy to raise. By the middle of 1973, *The Wall Street Journal* noted, "Utilities already gobble up more than 45 per cent of all funds raised in the capital markets. . . . From now on, . . . the utility companies will have to force on the market . . . 'more than half the net increase in total corporate debt likely to be raised by all industries,' according to Donald Mishara, a vice president of Smith, Barney & Co. and member of an advisory task force for the Federal

Power Commission." Between 1967 and 1975, the cost in constant dollars of building a nuclear power plant doubled. "Energy production makes the most rapidly growing demand for capital among all sectors of industry," Barry Commoner wrote in 1976. "The most immediate and intense expression of the capital shortage is in the electric power industry. In the last few years, a considerable proportion of planned installations, particularly of nuclear power plants, have been cancelled for want of capital."

Commoner argued that this want of capital would eventually make irrelevant the arguments about the controversial liquid metal-cooled fast breeder reactor. "The need for the breeder reactor," he said, ". . . has been removed by a kind of technological irony: the conventional reactors have themselves become so much more complex and therefore so much more expensive that the reduced cost of fuel which the breeder was supposed to achieve is much less economically significant. The cost of electricity produced by nuclear reactors now depends more on capital costs than on fuel costs, and the breeder is hardly the kind of power plant that can serve in this situation; compared with a conventional reactor, the breeder would reduce fuel costs but greatly increase capital costs. And so the breeder has been rendered obsolete."

Whether or not Commoner turns out to have been right about the breeder, he was certainly right about the capital requirements of less exotic nuclear plants. The difficulty of raising capital has probably done at least as much as the environmental movement to hinder the development of nuclear power. Still, the development of nuclear power continues, even in the shadows of the Columbia River dams. In a complicated way, electricity from the dams will actually make nuclear power a bit cheaper. The Bonneville Power Administration, in conjunction with the major Northwestern utilities, has worked out a plan under which the utilities will build many new nuclear generating plants. The BPA and the utilities claim that the plants will be needed to avert a power shortage. Critics claim that if all the plants now envisioned are actually built, they will produce a large and embarassing surplus of power, which the BPA and utilities will presumably dispose of—one doesn't want a surplus, after all—by luring in new industries and by selling power to California. The Seattle City Council decided in 1976 to prevent the city's municipally-owned utility from buying into two of these nuclear plants, on the grounds that the power simply wouldn't be needed within the next fifteen years, and that a 230-megawatt conservation program would serve the city just as well. It made no sense, they reasoned, to tie up capital in plants that would be producing more power than the city needed. The vote was for sufficiency instead of a temporary abundance. No other municipal government has ever made such a choice.

Nevertheless, based on their own projections that show the Northwest's demand for power rising immutably through the 1990s, the BPA and regional utilities are proceeding with their construction plans. The cost of power from the dams and power from the new plants will be averaged together, so that expensive electricity from the nuclear plants won't have to compete against cheap electricity from the dams. Ultimately, as power from all sources is pooled, the aluminum industry will get less of the power from the dams and pay more for what it gets. But the dams will keep the industry's electric bills down, and keep the industry itself in the Northwest.

Both the current sale of hydro power to the aluminum industry and the future production of nuclear power under the BPA's regional plan demonstrate the extent to which the flow of energy is determined by dollars.

While it is conventional and quite natural to discuss the problems of energy production in technical or environmental terms, one must also discuss them in terms of capital, or one has clearly missed much of the point. Things have multiple identities. The Columbia River is a natural phenomenon, and as such it simply *is*, governed by natural laws and oblivious to human interests. But the river has been incorporated into human economic systems. As an economic entity, it is above all a producer of commodities—whether those commodities happen to be fish or kilowatts. And it is governed partly by laws that have little to do with hydrology, biology or physics.

5. *The Arid Empire:*
Irrigating the West

As YOU drive east from Ephrata, the seat of Grant County, Washington, the landscape that unrolls beside your car is startlingly bleak: dry, humus-poor soil and a lot of sage, reaching to the horizon. After a while, low, stark buttes appear, and the road starts to rise. Past the cut-offs for Adrian, Stratford and Wilson Creek, you can turn right on a narrow, paved two-lane road that plunges due south through the rolling hills. On this land, sagebrush meets fertile fields right at the fence lines. On the cultivated side of the fence, you see massive irrigation devices, thick aluminum pipes that stretch on and on, suspended in the centers of the huge metal wheels on which they roll. A couple of miles down the road, you turn left onto gravel, pass more fields and wheel irrigators, and eventually come to a second gravel road. In the northwestern angle of the intersection of the two roads stands a weathered wooden farmhouse with a few trees and a small herd of farm machinery out in front. There, checking out one of the farm's two tractors, you find a husky, dark-haired man in his 30s named Bob Kissler. The wind is cold, and Kissler wears a dark, remarkably tattered jacket; after introductions, he looks down at it and says apologetically, "I'm trying to wear it out."

Kissler works this farm, some 640 acres of it, which belongs to his father, Fred Kissler, Jr., who bought it during the Depression. Like other farmers, he is concerned about the prices of his crops and the health of his machinery, planting times and plowing times, maintaining his line of credit and eradicating his weeds without the now-forbidden "high-volatile" herbicides. But unlike most other farmers—although not unlike many of his neighbors—Kissler has another, special concern: in twenty years or so, he is going to run out of water.

The water that courses through those big irrigators in Kissler's and his neighbors' fields is all pumped from deep underground. Kissler explains that the first well on his father's property, right behind the house, was drilled in the 1950s to a depth of little more than 500 feet. The next well went past 700 feet. The latest, in the field west of the house, is past 800 feet. Some people in the area have gone down more than 1500 feet, using oil-well-drilling apparatus to finish the job.

Sinking a deep irrigation well isn't cheap. One can count on paying $75 to $100 a foot for drilling, plus another $25,000 or so for a pump and pipe, plus a steep electric bill for running the pump. On the other hand, one can also count on a tripled yield per acre. In most parts of the country, people consider it normal for a farmer to get his moisture from the rains. In arid central Washington and the many western places like it, relying on the rains is known as "dry-land farming." Fred Kissler, Jr. bought that 640 acres for dry-land wheat farming. One can raise wheat there, but one must let the ground lie fallow every other year so it can accumulate enough moisture to support a crop. A dry-land wheat farm in the East High area, where the Kisslers live, will produce about twenty-five bushels per acre. An irrigated farm will produce about seventy-five. If wheat is selling at $5 a bushel, a 640-acre crop on irrigated land will be worth some $160,000 more than a 640-acre crop on dry land. With statistics like that, it isn't hard to see why, since the 1973 Russian wheat deal pushed farm prices up, people have been all but falling over each other in their rush to irrigate the East High area.

The trouble is, they are irrigating it from a pool of water that is only some 320 feet deep and has lain under that arid land for thousands of years. The more water is pumped out, the less water is left. In places, the water level has dropped 40 feet in a single year. The farmers in the area have now entered into a voluntary agreement with the Washington State Department of Ecology, which issues permits for well drilling, that none of them will drop the water level more than 30 feet over any three-year period. At that rate, no one figures that deep-well irrigation in the East High area has more than twenty years left, except for those farmers with the determination and the immense amount of capital needed to bore more than a quarter mile down into the next water-bearing layer. One might suppose that people would automatically conserve the only naturally occurring water in a virtual desert, but one would be wrong. Land and farm machinery have capital value. Water in the ground, like salmon in the sea, does not. Just as salmon are worth money only if you catch them, water is worth money only if you pump it. It is not conserving water but exploiting it that enables a man to pay off his capital investment and turn a profit while prices are still high.

What most people are hoping, Kissler says, is that within those twenty years, the federal government will have brought in water from the Columbia River, some 50 miles north. The government has already irrigated 540,000 acres to the west and south of Kissler's land, pumping water from behind Grand Coulee Dam and distributing it through more than 2,000 miles of canals that run all the way to the outskirts of Pasco, Washington, 180 miles south. Those 540,000 acres have been irrigated as the first stage of the Columbia Basin

Project, which was authorized by Congress in 1935. Kissler and his neighbors have been waiting for the second stage of the project, which may eventually bring the number of irrigated acres to more than one million and—more to the point—will transport water first to their portion of the East High area.

Kissler and his neighbors aren't the only people in the West who would like to see a little of the Columbia, which pours some 168 million acre feet of fresh water into the Pacific every year, flowing their way. (An acre foot, the standard unit of measure for irrigation purposes, is the amount of water needed to cover one acre to a depth of one foot.)

Throughout the arid regions of the West, people have a stake in continuing economic growth and extending human settlement in the middle of the desert. Without infusions of water, the cities and agricultural valleys of Southern California, like the booming residential tracts and retirement centers of Phoenix and Tucson, would be largely uninhabitable. A great deal of money is still waiting to be made in such places, and it won't be made without more water. "Both California and Arizona perceive that their [water] needs exceed their available supplies," a University of Washington geographer named Marion Marts has written, "and that shortages of water must not impede their manifest destiny." In the growth areas of the Southwest, people have been casting covetous glances at the Columbia River for years.

The history of moving water from place to place in the Southwest is discontinuous but very long. The remnants of great canals show that the Hohokam culture of Arizona was irrigating on a grand scale over 1300 years ago. The Hohokams disappeared—or perhaps transformed themselves into the Pimas and Papagos—but some Arizona Indians were irrigating when the Spaniards arrived in the 1500s. Some continued irrigating, in fact, until the white farmers who came in the late nineteenth century stole their water.

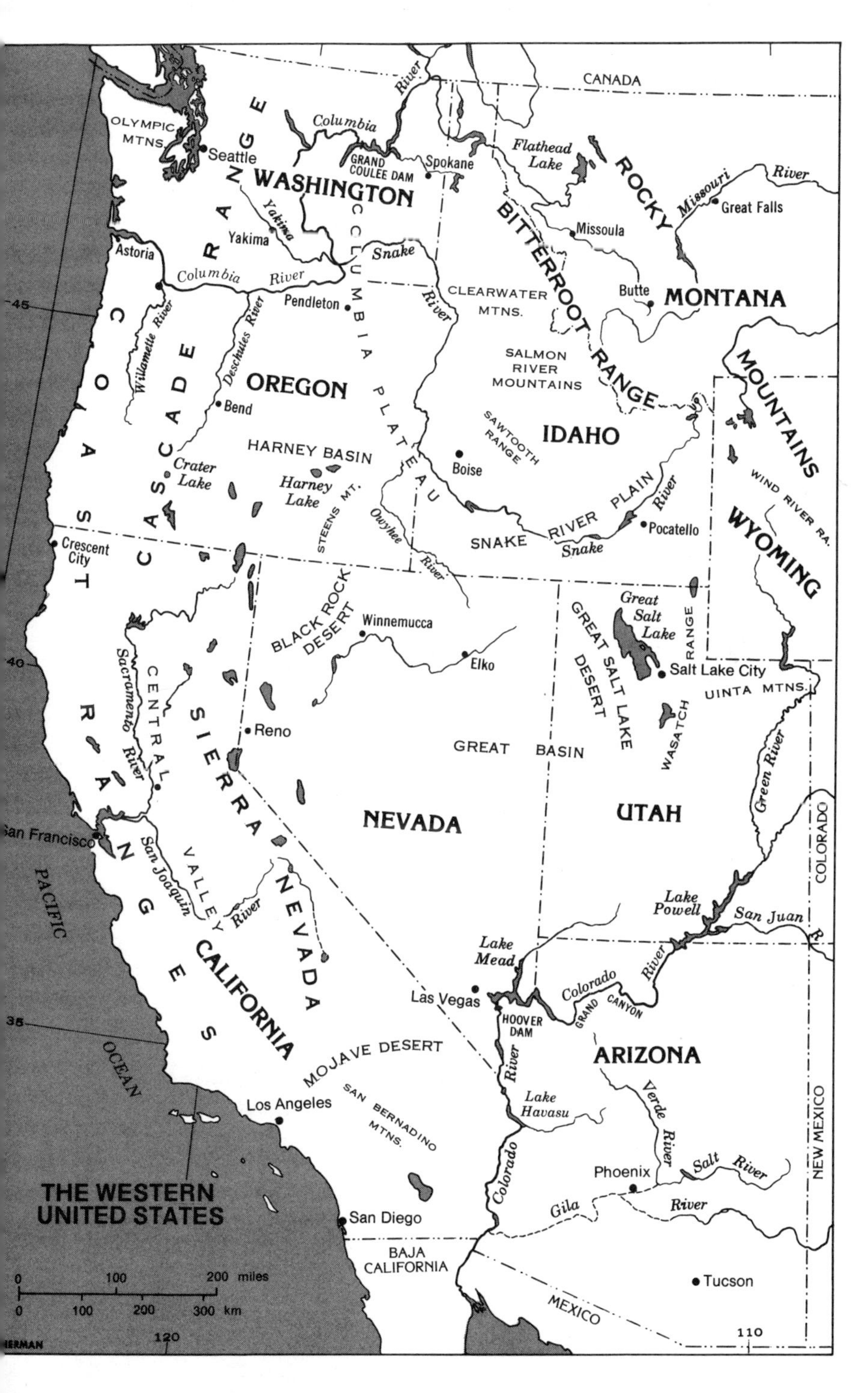

OLYMPIC MTNS.
Seattle
Columbia
GRAND COULEE DAM
Spokane
Flathead Lake
CANADA
ROCKY
Missouri
River
Great Falls
WASHINGTON
Yakima
Yakima
Snake
CLEARWATER MTNS.
Missoula
Butte
MONTANA
Astoria
Columbia
River
Pendleton
COLUMBIA
SALMON RIVER MOUNTAINS
BITTERROOT RANGE
Willamette River
Deschutes River
OREGON
Bend
River
SAWTOOTH RANGE
IDAHO
MOUNTAINS
WIND RIVER RA.
HARNEY BASIN
PLATEAU
Crater Lake
Harney Lake
STEENS MT.
Owyhee River
Boise
SNAKE
RIVER
PLAIN
River
Snake
Pocatello
WYOMING
CASCADE
Crescent City
BLACK ROCK DESERT
Winnemucca
Elko
Great Salt Lake
RANGE
Salt Lake City
UINTA MTNS.
Reno
GREAT SALT LAKE DESERT
WASATCH
CENTRAL
SIERRA
GREAT
BASIN
COAST
Sacramento River
NEVADA
UTAH
Green River
San Francisco
San Joaquin
VALLEY
NEVADA
River
COLORADO
PACIFIC
RANGES
Lake Powell
San Juan
R.
Lake Mead
CALIFORNIA
Las Vegas
Colorado
River
GRAND CANYON
OCEAN
MOJAVE DESERT
HOOVER DAM
Los Angeles
SAN BERNADINO MTNS.
River
Lake Havasu
ARIZONA
Verde River
NEW MEXICO
THE WESTERN UNITED STATES
Colorado
Phoenix
Salt
River
San Diego
Gila
River
Tucson
BAJA CALIFORNIA
MEXICO
0   100   200 miles
0   100   200   300 km
SHERMAN
120
110

The first whites who developed significant irrigation systems in the Southwest were the Mormons who came into the valley of the Great Salt Lake with Brigham Young. They diverted the streams from the surrounding mountains and hills and built a flourishing agricultural society in what had been a desert. With the Mormons as an example, the people who settled other arid portions of the West wanted to irrigate, too. In most cases, though, their means were limited. People tried to get land on the banks of rivers or streams. If they couldn't, the task of moving water to their land was generally too formidable for them to undertake. Just as the land was unusable without water, the water was in most cases unusable without enough capital to build irrigation works. Private irrigation companies, which had more capital than the individual farmers, did construct some sizable projects, but the companies retained absolute control over the distribution of water, and the farmers did not enjoy being at their mercy.

Major John Wesley Powell, the great explorer of the Colorado River, saw these private irrigation companies developing throughout the arid West, and noted in 1879 that, "the lands have no value without water. If the water rights fall into the hands of irrigating companies and the lands into the hands of individual farmers, the farmers then will be dependent upon the . . . companies, and eventually the monopoly of water rights will be an intolerable burden to the people."

In the late 1800s, a lot of people from the Western states started a movement—a crusade, for some of them—to get the federal government into the irrigation business. The federal government was richer than the farmers and less grasping than the private irrigation companies. By putting water on the land, it could make new homes for thousands and thousands of farm families who could no longer move west with the frontier. By reclaiming the desert, it could speed the settlement of this country's internal frontiers. "Reclamation" could also enable the land to produce a staggering agricultural bounty. As Walt Whitman had written in 1879 after a trip to Colorado, "That plain and prairie area (larger than any European kingdom) . . . is the inexhaustible land of wheat, maize, wool, flax, coal, iron, beef and pork, butter and cheese, apples and grapes—land of ten million virgin farms—to the eye at present wild and unproductive—yet experts say that upon it when irrigated may easily be grown enough wheat to feed the world."

At first, the reclamation people got nowhere. The Western states weren't united, and they hadn't figured out a way to overcome the Eastern states' understandable reluctance to subsidize them. But they persevered, and their effort became more sophisticated. First, the interested states banded together, forming a special-interest alliance for the purpose of steering a safe course through Congress that has proven as enduring as any of the dams it has subsequently persuaded the body politic to build (more enduring than the Teton Dam which collapsed in 1976). Senator Francis G. Newlands of Nevada came up with the idea of paying for federal irrigation projects with proceeds from the sale of federal lands in the states that would benefit, a neat way of countering Eastern objections. Theodore Roosevelt, the Rough Rider, with his emotional ties to the West and his desire to settle the internal frontier, was a strong supporter of reclamation. Mark Hanna, the quintessential Republican boss, was no ally of Roosevelt, but he supported it, too. The time was politically auspicious. The turn of the century was the heyday of frank American imperialism. Political leaders who believed destiny demanded that the Stars and Stripes fly over Cuba and the Philippines were presumably the right people before whom to dangle visions of a great empire in the American West. Newlands introduced the idea in 1901, and in 1902, Congress passed the Reclamation Act, which finally put the federal government into the irrigation business. (The states covered by the Act were and still are Arizona, California, Colorado, Idaho, Kan-

sas, Montana, Nebraska, Nevada, New Mexico, North Dakota, Oklahoma, Oregon, South Dakota, Texas, Utah, Washington and Wyoming.) The government has been in the
business ever since, building huge dams and mile after mile
of canal, moving water from river to plain and desert, making
possible the development of some of the most productive agricultural land in the world.

But despite some three-quarters of a century of reclamation, despite the expenditure of billions of dollars, the moist-
ening of whole counties, the transformation of magnificent
rivers and canyons into gigantic reservoirs, the arid West is
still not sated.

Take Arizona, where the Hohokams were building twenty-
five-mile-long canals at about the time the Moors conquered
Spain. The Gila River, which flows through southwestern
Arizona, supplied water to the Hohokams, to later Indians
and to the earliest Caucasian irrigation projects in the state.
So much water was dammed in and diverted from the Gila
that by 1920, the lower part of the river had virtually ceased
to flow, and farms along it were being abandoned. Man had
succeeded in watering the Arizona desert, but he had succeeded simultaneously in drying up central Arizona's principal river. Other sources of water were needed. One obvious
source was the underground water supply, into which irrigation wells were first drilled around 1915, and which has been
supplying water to Arizona farmers ever since. Another
source, as obvious to Southwestern farmers as the Columbia
is to Northwesterners, was the Colorado River. Water from
the Colorado now irrigates some 75,000 acres in Arizona via
the Wellton-Mohawk Canal, which funnels most of it into the
Gila Valley.

Neither the wells nor the canals have supplied enough
water to keep up with Arizona's demands. As Tucson and
Phoenix have mushroomed and the state's mining and manufacturing industries have grown, the demands on the water

supply have increased. Agriculture still takes more than 90 per cent of the water used in Arizona, but it is now competing for water against opponents that are much more highly capitalized. Both industries and municipalities can afford to buy up farms in order to get the farmers' share of the available water, and both have been doing so—which has caused Arizona's agriculturally-oriented legislative and banking leaders no slight distress.

Equally distressing has been the fact that farms, cities, mines and factories have been systematically depleting the state's groundwater, pumping water out faster than nature can replace it and lowering the water table just as steadily as the farmers in the East High area of central Washington are lowering theirs. Arizona's water table is sinking at a rate of some ten feet a year. Long before it disappears totally in most places, the cost of extracting water from it will become prohibitive for agricultural users.

Faced with a water supply that has always been inadequate and is now clearly dwindling, Arizona has pressed since the 1940s for a huge federal project to deliver water from the Colorado River in the northwest corner of the state to farms and cities in the middle of the state. For decades, this scheme, known as the Central Arizona Project, has been one of the great motherhood issues of Arizona politics. But outside Arizona, it has had to overcome strong political resistance.

Since the early days of this century, the states of the Southwest have agreed on the desirability of carving up the Colorado and disagreed about just how to do it. Originally, most of the states feared that California, which has always been bigger, richer and more voracious than its neighbors, would simply elbow everyone else out of the way. Therefore, to secure federal legislation that would permit irrigation of California and its "Lower Basin" companions, Arizona and Nevada, from the Colorado, those states had to sign a 1922 agreement that formally divided the river between them and the "Upper Basin" states of Wyoming, Colorado, Utah and New Mexico. Six years later, to get a federal commitment to build Boulder Dam and the All American Canal, California had to accept a formal division of water among the Lower Basin states.

California got the lion's share of the lower river, which begins at Lee Ferry, Arizona—a guarantee of up to 4,400,000 acre feet, against Arizona's 2,800,000 and Nevada's 300,000—but it wanted more. At the very least, it wanted to make sure that if there wasn't enough water to give each state its full share, California's share would not be reduced. To accomplish this, California tried, in effect, to reduce Arizona's share of the river. It did so by arguing that the Gila River, a tributary of the Colorado that is used entirely within Arizona's borders, should be counted as part of Arizona's share. Arizona naturally resisted, and the dispute eventually wound up in the Supreme Court. The Court ruled in 1963 that the Gila belonged entirely to Arizona, so it could not count as part of Arizona's share.

The Court's decision meant that Arizona was still entitled to enough of the Colorado to make the Central Arizona Project feasible. It also made California particularly eager to protect its own share. Legislation to authorize the Central Arizona Project came before Congress in 1968. And California's price for backing that legislation was an agreement that in case of a shortage, California could draw its entire 4,400,000 acre feet before a single drop could be diverted through the Project's aqueducts and canals.

Construction of the Central Arizona Project is underway. If all goes according to schedule, water will begin flowing through the aqueducts in 1985. But there won't be enough of it. Deep-well irrigation is depleting Arizona's water table at a rate of more than 2 million acre feet a year. At best, the CAP will deliver 1.2 million acre feet a year. At worst, when the

Upper Basin states, California and evaporation have taken their toll, Arizona won't get even that much. Evaporation is expected to take water from the four huge reservoirs and long desert canals planned for the Project at a rate of 100,000 acre feet a year. And there are indications that both the original compact for dividing the Colorado and the Bureau of Reclamation's original projections for the Central Arizona Project were based on uniquely high Colorado River flows that occurred in the early decades of this century. Analysis of tree-ring growth data—which give an accurate picture of past rainfall patterns—reveals that prior to the early 1900s, the last time such sustained heavy flows had occurred was in the early 1600s.

Arizona isn't the only Southwestern state in which the future looks rather parched. The same conflicts—agriculture versus municipal and industrial use versus outright scarcity—are endemic throughout the region.

The conflicts over water have been sharpened by the advent of big energy projects in the West. Big thermal power plants need a lot of cooling water. Coal mining, coal gasification and the production of oil from shale all require water, too. And the transportation of coal in slurry form would require the output of whole rivers.

The logical way out for Arizona and the other Southwestern states—logical, that is, in the context of some seventy-five years of large-scale federal irrigation projects—is to import water from other regions. As E. Roy Tinney, director of the Water Resources Center at Washington State University, has written, "When an ore deposit is exhausted, the mine is abandoned. . . . But with water and agriculture, there is a tendency to think along other lines. Farmers, businessmen and communities in the water-mining area assume that someone—presumably the federal government—will replenish their mine. . . . In much of the Southwest, there is no longer an adequate supply to develop additional acreage. Indeed, we are told that Arizona is forced to take land out of production because of the mined groundwater reservoir and the rapidly growing demand for municipal and industrial supply. . . . The Southwest's answer is to propose importation of waters from remote sources."

In the 1950s and 1960s, many schemes were hatched for transporting water from the damp Northwest to the arid Southwest. As a group, these schemes were probably among the grandest blueprints for rearranging nature that man has ever seriously sketched. Some involved tapping the Columbia or its tributaries. The more grandiose involved tapping the rivers of Alaska, northern British Columbia and the Yukon. One such scheme would have turned the Centennial Valley in Montana into a storage point for water flowing down from northern Canada; so much water would have filled the valley, calculations indicated, that the sheer weight of it would regularly have produced earthquakes reaching a magnitude of six on the Richter scale. Diversion of the far northern rivers would, of course, have been extremely expensive, even by 1960s standards. It would also have been highly unpalatable to the Canadians, and the idea seems to have been safely laid to rest. At least, it *seemed* to have been laid to rest until early 1977, after northern California had been shriveled by two solid years of drought. Speaking at a February press conference in Los Angeles, a representative of the engineering firm that had developed one of the huge water-moving schemes suggested that "with several crises hitting all at once . . . people may become interested again in this project." He said that water could begin flowing from the far north to the American desert within nine years. Arizona's Representative John Rhodes said the plan was an idea whose time had come.

The idea of diverting the far northern rivers may or may not be fully resurrected, but the idea of diverting the Columbia has never really died. Fast footwork and hard arm-twisting by Northwestern Senators have just kept it out of the spotlight for some years. In 1968, the House Interior Committee, chaired by Wayne Aspinall of Colorado, reported out a bill that not only authorized construction of the Central Arizona Project but also looked beyond the point at which the Colorado would be exhausted, and authorized federal studies of water transfers from other sources—like the Columbia. When the bill arrived at a House-Senate conference, that portion of it ran into trouble. The chairman of the Senate Interior Committee was Henry M. Jackson of Washington, who wasn't about to let the Colorado Basin states get their hands on the Columbia. Jackson and the other Northwestern Senators on the Interior Committee were in a very strong position. In return for their support of the Central Arizona Project, they got a ten-year moratorium on federal studies of any inter-basin water transfers.

The moratorium will expire in 1978, and after that, the Columbia will again be fair game. A recent issue of *Technology Review* has even introduced a brand new idea for exploiting it: construction of an underwater aqueduct, made of rubber, which could take water along the coast from the Columbia to California.

Russell D. Smith, manager of the Columbia Basin Project's South Irrigation District, has said that "whenever I go to California and talk with water resources people, the tops of their maps always have these red arrows pointing north, and next to the arrow it always says, '300 miles to the Columbia River.'" John Spencer, the Washington State Department of Ecology's assistant director for water resources, says there is a serious chance that the federal government will step in and decide that some of the Northwest's water could be put to better use someplace else. There are people in the Bureau of Reclamation who believe that a diversion of the Columbia or its tributaries would pay off in strictly economic terms, especially if the water were used to supply California's cities. (Sending more water to California might, of course, take some of the pressure off Arizona.)

In the areas that hope to benefit from big irrigation projects, great expectations are still very much in fashion. Occasionally, those expectations still reflect the original ideals of reclamation. As late as 1975, when Russell Smith was asked what the benefits of expanding the Columbia Basin Project would be, he answered, "Homes. Homes for people. It would enable more people to live the finest life there is: the life of an independent farmer." The theory has always been that federal reclamation should provide a living for small farmers. It has always been illegal for an individual land-owner to irrigate more than 160 acres with federally supplied water. That acreage limitation still exists, although people often circumvent it by putting 160 acres under the name of a spouse, which is legal, and also under the name of every conceivable child, cousin and hired man, which is not. In California, the subsidization of major agribusiness concerns with federal irrigation water in the Westlands area has become a significant issue.

Generally, people couch their expectations for federal irrigation projects in terms much less idealistic than Russell Smith's. They are more likely to point out that irrigating extra acres in the Columbia Basin, for example, will increase the agricultural output of the region, increase the local population up to thirty-fold, lead to the development of more local transportation and processing facilities, boost the business of every equipment, fertilizer and seed dealer in the region and pump many millions of dollars—thirteen dollars for every dollar invested in construction, according to one estimate—into the economy of Washington State.

People also suggest considerations that transcend the boundaries of places like Grant County, Washington. If the highly productive agricultural regions of the Southwest are vulnerable to drought, perhaps more water should be made available to them. If food is going to be the United States' main export in the foreseeable future, not to mention its chief non-military source of leverage on foreign governments, they say, the intensive cultivation of more land is clearly in the national interest.

Needless to say, there are many on-the-other-hands. One can point out, for example, that it is blatantly illogical to talk about putting more arid land under intensive cultivation while continuing to pave over naturally arable land in river valleys near cities. If it is desirable to irrigate more land in central Washington, it should be equally desirable to save what is left of the fertile river valleys near the coastal cities.

One can also ask if it is desirable to encourage the cultivation on currently arid land of such low-value crops as alfalfa—a major crop in many federally irrigated areas—which without *de facto* subsidization wouldn't return the cost of bringing water to them. Alfalfa, which is raised as a feed crop for cattle, can't even plausibly be considered a weapon in the battle against starvation in the underdeveloped world. But are even legitimate human food crops grown on irrigation projects likely to find their way to poor, starving people anyplace in the world? Does anyone seriously believe that growing more potatoes or sugar beets in central Washington, or growing more citrus in Arizona, is going to make life easier for poor people in Chad or Bangladesh? If continued water transfers are desirable or even necessary to keep people from starving, as some have suggested, then there should be some assurance that they will actually do that job: that exportable human food crops will be raised on the newly reclaimed land, and that those crops will find their way to hungry mouths, not to black-market warehouses or Russian cattle. If continued water transfers are desirable or necessary to soften the regional and national impact of serious drought, then again, there should be some guarantee that the land will be used to grow human food. The additional water should be transformed into food as directly as possible. It should not just be used to cushion the shock to local agriculture of the rapid growth of retirement centers, air-conditioned housing developments and industry in naturally arid places.

Finally, one might ask whether it is in the national or international interest to encourage the development of more fertilizer-intensive, energy-intensive agriculture in the United States. The whole point of putting water onto arid land is to increase the yield. Increasing the yield requires not only more water, but also more nitrogen fertilizer, and the need for nitrogen fertilizer increases more rapidly than the land's productivity. An acre of land that produces twenty-five bushels of wheat with x amount of fertilizer will require more than $3x$ to produce seventy-five bushels. And the production of each pound of nitrogen fertilizer requires 18.3 cubic feet of natural gas.

Fertilizer production is a major, if indirect, consumer of energy. The pumping of water for large irrigation projects consumes a lot of energy directly. The pumps required for the Central Arizona Project, for example, would consume enough energy to supply a city of 800,000 people.

The United States has never come to grips with these broad questions about the use of its fertile land. The nation has, however, evolved in ways that make the wisdom of big irrigation projects look increasingly shaky. After forty years, even completion of the Columbia Basin Project strikes some people less as a great national stride toward rural prosperity than as a highly questionable piece of local pork.

For purely economic reasons—don't spend today what you can just as easily spend tomorrow—the federal government decided to build the Columbia Basin Project in two stages. Once water was flowing through all of the planned first-stage canals, in 1967, Washington's powerful Senator Warren G. Magnuson got Congress to appropriate $100,000 to start the second stage. Magnuson kept getting money appropriated on and off for the next eight years, but the Nixon and Ford administrations kept refusing to spend it.

By the end of the 1960s, the post war federal cornucopia had begun to run dry. It was therefore more significant than it might once have been that any plausible amount charged farmers for the use of new Columbia River water wasn't likely to pay more than one-seventh of the direct cost of bringing that water to them. And, by the Office of Management and Budget's reckoning, there would also be indirect costs. All the water that comes past Grand Coulee Dam can now be used to generate electricity. Any additional water pumped onto the land from behind the dam will diminish the total amount of water available to generate power—an argument that can also be used against transfers of water to the Southwest.

Balanced against the cost and the power loss will be the production of additional food, but the Nixon Administration argued originally that the United States had no need to raise more food, so there was no need to irrigate more land. During the years when farmers were being paid to keep land out of production, that argument was hard to counter.

The argument also fit in well with the findings of the National Water Commission, a blue-ribbon group chosen by President Lyndon Johnson in 1968 to make a five-year study of American water use and policy. In 1973, the Commission reported that it was time for the federal government to stop giving water users a free ride. Barge companies should pay the full cost of dredging rivers and building and maintaining locks. And farmers should pay the full cost of constructing irrigation projects. The West has been won, the report argued, and what may once have been a perfectly rational policy has by now lost its rationale. The United States already has enough land under cultivation to feed its own population at least through the year 2000. Constructing more irrigation projects to grow more crops will constitute *de facto* subsidization of below-market-value sales, not to starving countries, but to countries perfectly able to pay their own way.

OMB seemed pleased to add the Commission's arguments to its own justifications for not spending money, but the private economic interests and government agencies whose income and power depended on big water projects weren't pleased at all. They wanted the report out of sight and out of mind as quickly as possible, and by and large, with the Nixon Administration already paralyzed by Watergate they were successful in putting it there. (The Commission's members were hardly shocked by this response. At around the time the report came out, one member remarked, "We've jumped right into the pork barrel.")

But they were not successful in changing the fact that—though the pork-barrel mentality may endure forever—reclamation doesn't seem to be very high on most people's lists of priorities any more. In a nation most of whose citizens were still busy wresting a living from the earth, the desirability of creating more productive farmland might seem clear. The choice might also be a simple one in a nation seriously committed to feeding the world. But in a nation only 4 per cent of whose citizens live on farms, a nation in which grain exports are widely resented as the cause of higher food prices, the choice isn't clear at all.

Certainly, the consensus that irrigating the arid lands of the West is good economic policy and settling people on those lands is good social policy would seem to be moribund at best. It was one thing for Teddy Roosevelt and the early reclamation crusaders to dream of building empires in the desert; it is quite another thing to entertain such dreams now, when a good many empires have already been built, and the business of empire-building has gone out of vogue.

Simultaneously, the costs of empire-building have increased enormously. By the time the Bureau of Reclamation's Teton Dam collapsed, the costs of nineteen big Bureau projects exceeded their authorized ceilings by $675 million. Inflation had already pushed the cost of the Central Arizona Project from $832 million to an estimated $2.1 billion. Representative William S. Moorhead of Pennsylvania had called the bureau's cost overruns "truly astounding."

As projects have grown more expensive, they have also begun to attract the attention of people who have no particular stake in their construction. This increased public scrutiny has tended to focus, in recent years, on a number of distressing facts: for instance, the fact that the Garrison Diversion Project, in North Dakota, will flood 218,000 acres of arable land in order to irrigate 250,000, and will pollute the waters of Manitoba in violation of an agreement between the U.S. and Canada.

Environmental concerns within the United States have developed into another major obstacle. While the damming and diversion of great rivers may once have seemed an unequivocal triumph over nature, it—and, for that matter, the consequent eradication of the desert—is now viewed by some people as a monstrous desecration. Environmentalists remember that some uniquely beautiful parts of the West, including the Cathedral in the Desert, have been flooded by water backed up behind Bureau of Reclamation dams. They are not inclined to smile on any more massive rearrangements of the landscape performed for man's economic benefit. Environmentalists may well be too quick to deprecate the desire of the farmer or engineer to make the desert bloom, the feeling of the grower or builder that there is, after all, a worthwhile job to be done. There is nothing base about a desire to make food crops grow—even for profit—or to combine river and desert in a way that will benefit human society. To produce is not necessarily less noble than to contemplate. Still, the environmental consciousness-raising of the 1970s is a fact. The idea that a great river flowing between its natural banks is not simply so much irrigation water wasted may be a new one, but it is very much with us.

Environmental objections and immense costs are the main things that Daniel Dreyfus, the Senate Interior Committee's staff water expert, has in mind when he says, "My personal, professional judgment is that there is not the chance of a snowball in hell" of seeing the Columbia River diverted to the Southwest. Dreyfus explains that while the idea has a definite subjective reality for certain people in both the Southwest and the Northwest—the Southwesterners' hopes and Northwesterners' fears are absolutely real—it could be translated into objective reality only through decisions reached on a national level, and the nation as a whole isn't likely to buy it.

Still, Dreyfus is willing to concede that things could change. The nation as a whole may not be noticeably eager to make the desert bloom in Washington or Arizona or anyplace else, but reclamation projects represent jobs and local income, as well as agrarian visions. When Jimmy Carter began his Presidency by trying to scrap the Central Arizona Project and other Bureau of Reclamation projects already in progress, Congress forced him to back down. Support for new reclamation projects may be harder to get, but high consumer prices, high unemployment or persistent drought might very well create such support in a hurry. "To attain high [economic] growth rates once again in the industrial world," W. W. Rostow wrote in early 1977, ". . . we shall certainly have to invest more to assure an adequate supply of water for irrigated agriculture in important areas of the U.S." A discussion of big new reclamation projects may not be entirely moot.

If it does turn out to be moot, if reclamation can't gain a new lease on life, then the United States will have reached a turning point of great significance to the West. With no additional water provided cheap by Uncle Sam, the Western states would have to do a much better job of divvying up the water they already have.

Traditionally, those states have allocated water largely on

the basis of a doctrine called "first in time, first in right," which can be translated as first-come-first-served. They have made no effort to differentiate among the social values of potential uses or users. And they have granted permits for the use of water in perpetuity, so that anyone who has a right to use water now can expect to retain that right forever.

As competition for the existing water has increased, officials of those states have begun discussing changes in their systems of issuing water permits, and Washington—after controversy and delays—has even made a significant change. In 1975, the governors of both Washington and Utah backed legislation that would have imposed time limits on all new permits for the use of large amounts of water, and would have enabled the states to choose among prospective users in the future. One incentive for introduction of the Utah legislation had been the prospect of massive energy developments in that state. The officials who backed the legislation were by no means hostile to energy development, but they were concerned that a big energy company would be able to come in, buy up the necessary water rights for the operation of, say, a coal gasification plant and then, after the plant had outlived its usefulness, retain its right to a sizeable share of Utah's scarce and precious water.

In Washington, the main reason for the legislation was evidently the governor's realization that if all the people who had applied for water permits actually received them, and if all the permit holders then simultaneously tried to exercise their permit rights, not even the middle stretch of the Columbia would supply enough water to go around. Furthermore, 95 per cent of the water applied for would have gone to just 5 per cent of the applicants.

As the conflicts over water use multiply, the logic of Washington's move should become increasingly clear. A definite national rejection of further reclamation projects will only increase its clarity.

Of course, this society is no more accustomed to winnowing out uses of water than it is to winnowing out uses of electricity. Besides, to choose among prospective users of water is to condemn certain prospective users to economic extinction. That is not an attractive prospect. It is much more attractive to think about bringing in new water from someplace else.

This is not entirely a matter of individual or sectional greed. It is not easy to decide that a man like Bob Kissler should no longer be able to make a living from the land, that the irrigated fields of the East High area should be given back to the desert. Surely, a nation that can afford to bail out an imprudent aircraft manufacturer can afford to help a group of hardworking, independent farmers. Surely, 50 or 100 or 150 miles isn't terribly far to move the water that those farmers need to survive. But where does one draw the line? What about the hardworking farmers 1500 miles away? Should the natural resources of half a continent be altered to keep them afloat? Does the Southwest, a region that depends on infusions of water, have any right to expect its rapid, profligate growth to be subsidized by more infusions? Must the body politic insure the profitable coexistence of cotton farms, copper mines and Sun City? Must the highest-spraying fountain in the world, located in the middle of an Arizona housing development, be kept spraying?

The Columbia River is awesomely real. No one who has stood in the new powerhouse at Grand Coulee and felt the concrete building rumble with the force of water rushing underfoot can easily doubt that reality. But it also perpetuates a comforting illusion: that we don't really have to take all this conservation business seriously, because there is still more and more and more. The U.S. cavalry may be gone, but some people in the land of Hollywood and the transplanted London Bridge still expect to see water come flowing over that distant hill, just in time to save them from certain death.

6. Public Domain—Private Profit

ONE recent Christmas season, a friend of mine attended a dinner party at the home of a Northwestern timber baron. As everyone sat down for dinner, my friend found himself in conversation with his host, suggesting, as he recalled later, that perhaps the National Forests shouldn't simply be sold off to private industry. It seemed a modest enough suggestion at the time, but before my friend had a chance to eat his soup, he was asked to leave the house.

The timber baron's obviously strong conviction that the nation's forests exist chiefly for the economic benefit of anyone in a position to exploit them is hardly new. Carl Schurz wrote in 1889, that when he became Secretary of the Interior, "I observed the notion that the public forests were everybody's property, to be taken and used or wasted as anybody pleased, everywhere in full operation. I observed enterprising timber thieves not merely stealing trees, but stealing whole forests. I observed hundreds of saw mills in full blast, devoted exclusively to the sawing up of timber stolen from the public lands.

"I observed a most lively export trade going on from Gulf ports as well as Pacific ports, with fleets of vessels employed in carrying timber stolen from the public lands to be sold in foreign countries, immense tracts being devastated that some robbers might fill their pockets. . . . I deemed it my duty to stop at least the commercial depredations upon the property of the people. And to that end, I used my best efforts. . . .

"What was the result? No sooner did my attempts in that direction become known, than I was pelted with telegraphic dispatches from the regions most concerned, indignantly inquiring what it meant that an officer of the Government dared to interfere with the legitimate business of the country! Members of Congress came down upon me, some with wrath in their eyes, others pleading in a milder way, but all solemnly protesting against my disturbing their constituents in this peculiar pursuit of happiness."

The kind of wholesale plunder that Schurz observed vanished long ago. But many people believe that the public domain is still being plundered (albeit less openly), that some of the plunder is nourishing an export trade, and that the plundering is vital to some local economies. In fact, elements of Schurz's observations appear in all the current conflicts over the use of the National Forests.

The issue isn't whether or not industry should be able to profit from cutting and selling the public's trees. Virtually no one argues that it should not. A few would prefer to see all the trees in the National Forests left to live out their natural lives and eventually rot back into the soil, but most, presumably, would rather have lumber for framing houses, pulp for making paper, the income and jobs that the processing of "forest products" provides. The National Forests are an aesthetic resource for the nation, to be sure, but they are an economic resource, too, and that means somebody has to cut some of the trees. The body politic isn't equipped to take to the woods with chainsaw and bulldozer—any more than it is equipped to drill for oil on the outer continental shelf or strip-mine federal lands for coal—and that leaves the job to private industry. No one suggests seriously that the government put itself into the logging business.

Only private industry has the tools needed to exploit the nation's forests, but private industry is not uniquely equipped to make economic decisions about them. And private and public interests do not necessarily coincide. The National Forests are public property, and some people suggest that industry is profiting from them to the detriment of the public at large: the economic benefits are going elsewhere; the forests are being altered beyond any plausible legislative intent; and, in the long run, the forests are being systematically destroyed.

Of course, neither the industry nor the Forest Service concedes that the forests are being destroyed, or that their judicious use fails to benefit the American people.

The arguments are hard to resolve, but they are well worth following: The United States contains some 770 million acres of forest, of which some 500 million acres are classified as commercial (suitable for logging). The National Forests contain 187 million acres, of which only 90 to 97 million are classified as commercial. But the commercial portions of the National Forests currently supply 25 per cent of the nation's annual timber harvest and contain some 50 per cent of the nation's softwood inventory.

One might infer from those statistics that the federal government owned most of the United States' best tree-growing land, but actually, just the opposite is true. Not even in the highly-productive "Douglas fir" region of western Washington and Oregon does the federal government own most of the best land. Millions of acres of forest are privately owned, and those acres include most of the better soil. Private ownership of that soil is a legacy of the late nineteenth century, of a time during which the public domain was not only being plundered, as Schurz described, but also being systematically parcelled out to private owners.

In the Northwest and elsewhere, enormous grants of land were the inducement that the federal government offered to private entrepreneurs for the construction of transcontinental railroads. The Northern Pacific Act, which President Abraham Lincoln signed into law in 1864, was an example. In exchange for a railroad from St. Paul to Puget Sound, it offered all odd-numbered sections of land for twenty miles on either side of the track in states, and for forty miles on either side of the track in territories, including Idaho, Montana and Washington. When the Northern Pacific Company laid the rails, it got the land. Much of that land is still owned by a handful of corporations.

In retrospect, the grant may seem an excessive price to have paid for rail lines over which Amtrak now talks of curtailing service because there are so few paying passengers. To see both Weyerhaeuser and the Burlington Northern listed among the country's top eight corporate landowners and to realize that much of their holdings derive from the original grant gives one pause. It gives some people more than pause. Harvey Manning has written in *Not Man Apart* that "Weyerhaeuser and Pack River and the other blackguards 'own' that . . . land solely by 'right' of theft, their burglar tools being, in this case, mainly the Northern Pacific land grant. . . . I live in constant fury knowing that fourteen companies (or, if you check out interlocks, a half-dozen) won 5,000,000 acres of Washington forest land—and the *best* acres for growing trees, the nineteenth-century pirates being fastidious."

But during the third quarter of the nineteenth century, although the railroad builders were known to be both rich and greedy, both corrupting and corrupt, the nation as a whole seemed willing to pay a high price in order to get the transcontinental rail lines laid. As Henry Adams observed in his autobiography, "The generation between 1865 and 1895 was . . . mortgaged to the railroads, and no one knew it better than the generation itself."

That generation put much of the nation's best tree-growing soil into private hands. The National Forests wound up with the left-overs. But if one is talking about current supplies of harvestable timber, the quality of soil is somewhat beside the point. Most of the big trees on the fertile, easily accessible low lands, which are chiefly under private ownership, were logged off long ago. It is in the National Forests, where the slopes are steep and the loggers haven't yet been, that most of the remaining big timber is to be found. One first-growth Douglas fir trunk weighing in at ten tons equals a lot of younger trees grown on more hospitable terrain. It is because the National Forests hold most of the remaining big trees that they account for so much of the annual supply.

No one suggests seriously that those big trees are going to disappear overnight. Certainly, no one today seems quite as pessimistic as Theodore Roosevelt was in 1907 when he told Congress that "so rapid has been the rate of exhaustion of timber in the United States and so rapidly is the remainder being exhausted that the country is unquestionably on the verge of a timber famine. . . . The present annual consumption is certainly three times as great as the annual growth; and if the consumption and growth continue unchanged, practically all our lumber will be exhausted in another generation." At the very least, things seem to have improved.

The next generation will have lumber and will also have forests, of a sort. How much lumber and what kinds of forests are the great unknowns.

In recent years, the timber industry and the Forest Service have concluded that the nation can obtain the largest continual supply of timber by treating an acre of trees like an acre of wheat, harvesting and replanting the area at regular intervals. This "clearcutting" of entire tracts is hardly new. With one interruption, which began during the Depression and lasted through World War II, it has been the standard method of harvesting timber in the National Forests of the Northwest. It is easier and cheaper to cut all the trees in a given area than to cut selectively and have to snake the cut logs out through a growth of standing trees. But now, both the industry and the Forest Service maintain that cheapness isn't the only virtue of clearcutting. Because the economics are better, they say, the company doing the cutting can afford to use marginally profitable wood that might otherwise be left in the forest to rot. Clearcutting also requires fewer miles of logging roads and results in less accidental breakage of otherwise-usable trees. Finally, clearcutting makes biological sense: young trees grow faster if they can have unobstructed sunlight; they are less likely to be crowded out by commercially undesirable species; and they are being grown in the way that nature has grown them after clearing the land with fire and storm for thousands of years.

The appeal of clearcutting isn't visual, of course. You can ride an Amtrak observation car through the Cascade Mountains and hear, not bearded environmentalists, but retired railroad men and their wives expressing horror at the naked slopes. Not even the advocates of clearcutting claim that a mountainside of stumps is a thing of beauty.

Among environmentalists, clearcutting arouses very strong negative feelings. Aesthetics aren't the environmentalists' only interest, but perhaps those feelings are so strong because clearcutting clashes violently with most people's image of a forest. To most of us, a forest is an enduring stand of trees from which individual trunks may be removed by wind or disease, chain saw or ax, but which never vanishes in its entirety. To the timber industry, though, a commercial forest is often a plot of land on which trees are periodically sown and harvested, without ever growing large enough to create what one industry forester has described as the "cathedral effect" found in an old natural forest. The two images have little in common.

Beyond—or perhaps not entirely beyond—the problem of conflicting images lie more concrete criticisms of the new forestry as applied to the old National Forests. "What emerges from modern research," Ivan Doig has written in

Pacific Search, "instead of the casual notion that any Douglas fir forest anywhere needs sizable open patches for its seedlings to take hold, is that *some* stands of Douglas fir, in *some* locations, can thrive that way. . . . [Here] is the evaluation of Dr. David M. Smith, the Yale forestry professor whose *The Practice of Silviculture* is the field's standard textbook: 'It is actually fortunate that the routine of clearcutting, burning and seeding or planting of Douglas fir has worked at all. In most instances, the optimum environment for young Douglas firs is found underneath partial shade.' "

Former Secretary of the Interior Walter Hickel has written that, "undoubtedly, there are situations in which clearcutting of trees is justified, but there are many cases in which it represents an abuse of a resource. . . . Does it make sense to cut a 3-year-old tree, a 30-year-old tree and a 300-year-old tree all at the same time just because they are standing next to each other?

"The real argument for clearcutting," Hickel maintained in his autobiographical book *Who Owns America?*, "is that it is cheaper to do it that way and take a chance on the forest replenishing itself." Critics of the industry claim that the forest isn't replenishing itself rapidly enough: that the industry isn't growing trees at a rate that makes up for the old-growth timber it is cutting. In fact, they say, the industry is using old trees from the National Forests to make up the difference between growth and harvest on its own "intensively managed" lands. To quote Harvey Manning, whose rhetoric may be extreme but whose convictions are widely shared, "Weyerhaeuser and the rest of the bandit gang, behind a smokescreen of magazine ads and TV commercials bragging about nonexistent corporate 'tree farms,' are overcutting 'their own' lands and meanwhile, for the sake of one last fix, are besieging the National Forests." (Weyerhaeuser is probably the most statesmanlike of the big companies, but it tends to turn up first on lists of corporate evildoers.)

"The truth is," Gordon Robinson, a former chief forester for the Union Pacific, has written in *Not Man Apart,* that "if the timber industries had actually practiced forestry on their own lands, they would not be fighting for our public timber. . . . In 1970, the most recent year for which we have statistics, 48 billion board feet of softwood timber was removed from the U.S.'s commercial forest land. But we grew only 40 billion board feet. That same year, removals from the national forests were 12.7 billion board feet, but growth was only 8.6 billion board feet. . . . In the Douglas fir region, both the Forest Service and the Bureau of Land Management (BLM) are selling timber under one standard of measurement while estimating future yields under another. The minimum-sized tree counted in present inventories of standing timber measures 12 inches in diameter, and its volume is calculated to an 8-inch diameter at the treetop. . . . Estimates of future yields, however, which are used for calculating allowable cuts, include minimum-sized trees only 7 inches in diameter measured to a 5-inch top. The difference in volume between these two standards of measurement in a second-growth stand will be about 40 per cent of the total; the second 'drop' will be 40 per cent smaller than the first. So while the BLM says it is selling timber in annual amounts that will never decline, there will actually be a decline of as much as 40 per cent in the sustained yield, once the present forests (which have taken centuries to mature) have been liquidated. The next stand will be smaller and much less valuable. The Forest Service makes use of the same rationalization, but in a more involved way."

Critics of the Forest Service, who include not only organized environmentalists but Congressmen and corporate foresters, also point out that the Forest Service may be in no position to apply corporate methods to federal lands. Even if one accepts the virtues of industry's "intensive" forest management at face value, the success of intensive management will depend at least partly on the quality of soil and the amount of cash that can be employed. The Forest Service is not well supplied with either soil or cash. Some soil within the National Forests is good, but some is clearly not. The Stanford Research Institute has said that, "part of the relatively low net growth on Forest Service lands in the Pacific Northwest reflects the fact that the Forest Service has a high proportion of . . . lands with a comparatively low potential for growing timber within its ownership."

The critics also agree that the service has been chronically underfunded, and has been kept in the untenable position of managing a living resource with a life span of many decades on a budget that changes from year to year. Funding has a lot to do with the potential effectiveness of industry's "intensive management" system. For one reason or another, tree-planting often fails. If a corporation plants seedlings that don't survive, it has the option of going back and planting a second or third time. The Forest Service may have money to plant only once. At this point, it is administering millions of acres that need reforestation. "Most students of forestry realize," Representative Lloyd Meeds has said, "that the cut [of timber] from the National Forests can be increased—but only . . . if the capital funds are assured. . . . [But] making those investments is not particularly attractive to the budget people downtown. The Chief of the Forest Service revealed in 1973 that he had asked OMB for $854 million, and that OMB had allowed him to come to Congress and beg for $457 million."

However underfunded the Forest Service may have been, its record includes sins of commission as well as of omission. By permitting clearcutting in the National Forests, for example, it was acting illegally for decades. The Organic Act of 1897, which set up the Forest Service, explicitly forbade the cutting of any trees that were not either dead or fully mature and had not been previously marked. Its provisions were successfully ignored until 1975, when the Fourth Circuit Court of Appeals ruled that if the Forest Service permitted clearcutting in West Virginia's Monongahela National Forest, it would be breaking the law.

The Forest Service extended that ruling to all National Forests under the court's jurisdiction, reducing the harvest for the rest of that fiscal year from a planned 285 million board feet to 30 million. At the end of 1975, another federal court applied the same logic to southeastern Alaska's Tongass National Forest.

The economic impact of those court decisions was potentially vast. Even before the Alaskan decision was rendered, people began speculating about what would happen if clearcutting were banned in all the National Forests of the United States. Various interested parties estimated that such a ban would make the harvesting of from 40 to 70 per cent of the Forests' commercial timber economically unfeasible. The National Plywood Association—a knowledgeable party but hardly a disinterested one—claimed that 12,700 forest industry jobs would disappear in Washington and Oregon alone.

The collection of environmental groups that had initiated the Monongahela National Forest suit weren't after a nationwide ban on clearcutting. What they wanted was an incentive for Congress to reform the Organic Act, and that is exactly what they got. Two separate bills for the reform of the act were drafted and introduced in early 1976. One, introduced by Senator Hubert Humphrey and drafted under the guidance of the Forest Service, essentially proposed to let the service do what it thought best. The other, introduced by Senator Jennings Randolph of West Virginia, called for more fundamental changes, requiring any proposal for logging in a National Forest to go before an interdisciplinary review board and limiting clearcutting to areas of no more than twenty-five acres. Congress passed a stiffened version of the Humphrey bill.

The industry's critics had naturally preferred the Randolph

bill, while the industry and the Forest Service naturally had not. Randolph himself, an old New Dealer but hardly a radical, had been interested in clearcutting since the mid-1960s. As an aide explained it, "When he saw 400- to 500-acre clearcuts and the rivers in West Virginia running muddy for seven weeks at a stretch, that was too much."

The industry argued, however, that even as far as his native West Virginia was concerned, Randolph was working under a delusion. Robert Witter, Weyerhaeuser's manager of land and timber resources said, for example, that even in the kind of mixed-species hardwood forest with which Randolph is familiar, clearcutting is a perfectly appropriate way to harvest trees, that the Monongahela National Forest itself is no eternal grove but an even-aged stand of trees only about fifty years old that grew there after the area was totally cleared by logging and fire.

Clearcutting may be nature's way, but in the good old days, when nature was the only one doing the clearcutting, a cycle of forest growth took a long time. Lightning did not strike regularly every forty or fifty years. And the seeds that grew to become the next forest weren't selected to produce the greatest number of board feet in the fewest possible years.

What man has done has been to put certain large tracts of forest land onto a production schedule: if all goes well, the land will yield so many board-feet of such and such a kind of timber every so many years. Some of the consequences of this production system are unknown and, in the short run, unknowable. Others seem obvious. In the Northwest, one of the obvious consequences has been the hustling toward extinction of mature western red cedars.

The western red cedar has never been the dominant species anywhere in the Northwest, but it has been there, inhabiting the moist valleys of the coast, and it has played a unique part in the coast's human history. The wood of the cedar is straight-grained, easy to work and exceedingly rot-resistant. It was the wood used for the great carved totem poles of the Northwest Coast Indians, and the long, sea-going canoes from which those Indians hunted fish and whales. Whites split the cedar into shakes and shingles and fence posts, sawed it into boards for silos and siding. Shingle and shake mills have provided the main source of income for small coastal towns since the beginning of white settlement.

The trouble is that to produce a wood so straight-grained and long-lasting, nature requires a long time. A mature cedar, a tree with a large enough cross-section to be of commercial value, requires 200 to 250 years of growth. No industry is going to plant trees on which it can't hope to profit for at least two centuries. Consequently, while the timber companies willingly cut cedar—the wood is still valuable for lumber, shakes and shingles, and some is shipped to Japan—they replant the cutover land in hemlock or Douglas fir. This is corporate policy, and for any corporation operating over a finite span of time, it is a rational one.

Nor should the growing scarcity of mature cedar come as any surprise. During the mid-1700s, a Swedish naturalist named Peter Kalm visited the American colonies and wrote that in Philadelphia, "the houses are covered with cedar shingles. The wood is very light, rots less than any other, and for that reason is exceedingly good for roofs, for it is not too heavy for the walls and will last forty or fifty years. . . . At present this kind of wood is almost entirely gone." In the Northwest, people have been predicting cedar's imminent demise as a commercial species since at least the 1920s. So far, the region's mills keep grinding out cedar shingles, shakes and boards at a largely undiminished rate. Still, no one doubts the end will come. Only the date is in doubt. Not all cedar will disappear, but except in National Parks and on the land of private owners crotchety enough to prefer living trees to money in the bank, cedars big enough to turn into totem poles or canoes, thick enough to split for shakes or shingles, tall enough to ultimately form 200-foot snags standing in the dark swamps for generations will no longer exist. Explaining that cedars will naturally seed themselves in areas replanted with Douglas fir, an industry forester said not long ago that, "cedar won't disappear—just *big* cedar."

Just as industry's current management systems will inevitably restrict the diversity of species within a forest, so some people worry that it will restrict genetic diversity within a given species. "Why . . . do the tallest firs, pines, spruces, hemlocks, redwoods and larches all rise along the Pacific Coast of North America?" Roy R. Silen, principal plant geneticist at the Pacific Northwest Forest and Range Experiment Station's Forestry Sciences Laboratory has written in *Pacific Search*. "From a vantage point of three decades in forest research, I believe the key to this wealth of timber is more than a matter of soil and moisture. Taken together, the genes of our twenty-two commercial species of western conifers seem to me to constitute our vital basic resource. And unless we recognize the magnificent quality of this gene pool, we may needlessly risk pauperizing or destroying it as man begins to alter it along the lines of his customary philosophy of genetic improvement. . . .

"Right now, some investment in tree improvement programs of one kind or another has been made in seven out of every ten acres of commercial forest land in the Pacific Northwest. The history of man's effects on other gene pools is a warning to us that once begun, any alteration tends to become more and more extensive. . . .

"Picture the landowner's choice of alternatives in reforestation if some forest geneticist should produce a refined strain that promises to give a 50 per cent gain in production. Will that landowner have any long-range concern for his present forest gene pool? Can he compete if he resists using the new strain?

"Yet the already existing strain, genetically tuned to its

own local land form and ecosystem and probably growing at the rate that long-term extremes of the environment will permit, may well be superior in most ways. And much is at stake whenever we thoughtlessly discard a locally adapted, well-buffered, multi-species gene pool. In forestry the crop is long-lived, and it may take the length of a human lifetime just for any mistakes in the altered gene balance to show up."

If you leave a tree with natural genes in a natural forest until it has lived out its natural life, what happens is exactly what the proponents of clearcutting say happens: the tree dies and rots. Thousands of board-feet of lumber, thousands of dollars of potential income, ultimately disappear into the forest floor. From an economic point of view, it is a colossal waste. From nature's point of view, however, nothing is ultimately wasted, and all those tons of unused lumber become tons of fertilizer, which nourish future generations of trees. Can the forests do without this nourishment? Industry foresters believe they can. A report on *The Effects of Clearcut Harvesting on Forest Soils,* put out by the American Forest Institute, observes that "trees contain rather small amounts of nutrients in comparison to the amounts in the soil. . . . A study in Washington State showed that about 10 per cent of the available soil nitrogen was accumulated in Douglas fir trees growing on the study site for thirty-five years. . . . The major part of the trees' nutrient content was in the needles, twigs, branches and roots, and normally all of this material remains on the site after the harvest. Rainfall alone annually adds about two pounds of nitrogen per acre to these watersheds, in itself enough to replace more than half of the thirty-five-year-old Douglas firs described above. But even this addition from rainfall is small, however, when compared to the input from biological fixation of atmospheric nitrogen." The report says that no studies of clearcutting have found a serious depletion of soil nutrients that was more than short-lived.

No one knows, however, if all the important elements have been tested for, and no extensive tests have been done on cycles involving old-growth Douglas firs. "Most major forest soil research has been conducted in the United States only since 1948," the report points out, and "studies of nutrient cycling began about ten years ago."

A couple of years ago, I was present when someone asked a group of industry representatives if, in fact, the soils could withstand frequent clearcutting over a period of years. Oh yes, he was assured, there seemed no doubt of that; perhaps some types of soil in some areas would suffer under that kind of system, but research indicated that in the Douglas fir region, the soils would not be harmed. If you wanted proof, after all, you could just look at nature's own track record: ever since the last ice age there had been periodic lightning fires that cleared large areas, and the forests had certainly survived.

That might be so, I suggested, but nature hadn't done it every forty or fifty years, and neither had man for very long. I couldn't believe that the industry or anyone else could speak quite so authoritatively about the long-term effect on soils.

No, he conceded, that was true; the best anyone could do was make an educated guess.

Soil erosion is a good deal easier to verify. Randolph and other critics can talk about the rivers below clearcuts running brown, but the industry and Forest Service have always claimed that done properly, on the proper terrain, clearcutting does not make soil erode. It can actually protect soil against erosion, they say, and in any case, tends to do far less damage than the extra miles of logging road that selective cutting requires.

Ultimately, Robert Witter of Weyerhaeuser argues, the only choice in the National Forests is between intensive management of a relatively small area and less-intensive management of a much larger one. The larger the area from which trees must be cut, the smaller the area that can be left entirely for other uses. However much land is logged, the yield of wood must be the same because the nation must assure itself of a steady supply of lumber and other wood products at a reasonable price. "This is a consumer issue," he explains, and he is probably right: among the public at large, the technicalities of forest management arouse much less interest than the price of two-by-fours.

The economic arguments over forest management can be carried to absurd lengths. The framing for houses is one thing, the flow of wood products that fill the country's municipal dumps quite another. Oregon's state forester was quoted in 1974 as saying, "We cannot maintain our forests as landscape gardens if we want adequate, low-cost toilet paper in the future."

Still, economics permeate all decisions made about the forests. Ivan Doig has written, "When the economic factors of the Depression pointed in favor of selective cutting, it became official policy in the Northwest's National Forests. When the economic considerations of better market conditions and the depletion of privately-owned timber began pointing toward the 'efficiency' of taking out entire stands of timber, clearcutting became the policy once again. All in all, that [experience] might serve as a classic lesson that disputes over use of our forests are not going to be decided on ecological merit alone."

Some, presumably, are not going to be decided on ecological merit at all. One such dispute involves the exporting of logs from the Douglas fir region of the Northwest. It has long been an article of faith among many residents of the Douglas fir region that by shipping logs to Japan before American mills and millworkers have had a shot at them, the timber industry has been "exporting jobs." Like the hostility to foreign fishing fleets, the opposition to log exports has an ironic ring of anti-colonialism. Here are people living in a resource-rich area who resent seeing the resource carted off by foreigners and would prefer to have it processed at home by native labor.

The economic facts about log exports are anything but clear. Millworkers' unions naturally support a ban on exports. Longshore unions, whose members load the logs being shipped to Japan, oppose it. The timber industry claims that in Western Washington alone, some 16,000 jobs depend on log exports. The industry argues that there is no reason to believe Japan would be willing to import more finished lumber instead of logs. Also, the industry says it uses income from exports to finance the extensive reforestation that guarantees the future of forest-based employment in the Northwest.

The industry's opponents don't buy those arguments. They maintain that the Northwest really is exporting jobs, and that the industry itself is practicing "cash-flow forestry," using income from denuding the Northwestern forests to set up timber operations in the Southeast and abroad. Congressman Lloyd Meeds says that "the cash flow generated by [exports] can be invested as a company decides. . . . The large companies can translate their profits into reforestation in a given area . . . or . . . can translate the cash flow into timber acquisition and mill construction in some other part of North America or the world. I would suggest that a reading of *Moody's Industrial Digest* shows that forest companies are constantly buying up timber and mills in various areas of the globe."

Finally, Meeds and other people who oppose log exports have pointed to studies conducted by the Forest Service, the Stanford Research Institute (SRI) and the Library of Congress which all indicate that Northwestern timber reserves are declining, that forest-based employment will decline with them, and that log exports are part of the problem. The Forest Service has estimated that between 1970 and

2000, the timber supply in the Douglas fir region will decline by 3.821 billion board feet, while forest-based employment will be cut by almost half. SRI used a lot of the Forest Service's data, but suggested that "Forest Service projections of the supplies of timber available from private lands—particularly in the West—in the year 2000 may be overly optimistic." SRI's own analysis of the situation was that, "if recent trends of cut and growth continue, the total private timber inventory in the region will be drastically reduced over the next two decades and—without offsetting increases in the annual harvest of public timber—the total annual harvest of softwoods in the region will decline." A senior SRI official once told me with amusement that on the day the Stanford report came out, the vice-president of a major timber company phoned him repeatedly, hanging up in frustration each time because he was unable to talk for more than a few minutes without breaking down and shouting curses into the phone.

In its more rational moments, the industry has been able to pick holes in the various studies. When the Library of Congress study came out, an industry official claimed that by using the same logic, its author might have concluded that the next harvest would wipe out corn in Iowa. Despite such criticism, the studies provide the industry's critics with powerful ammunition.

Meeds, for example, has quoted Forest Service figures which indicate that a thousand board feet of timber exported as unprocessed logs generate only 23 to 38 per cent as many man-hours of labor as the same amount of timber processed in the United States. A forestry expert on Meeds' staff, Mark Hauser, has written, "The SRI report adds that national forest management has become too political owing to the fact that each interest group perceives a threat in proposals to expand management beyond the interest group's primary concern. SRI really hits the nail here, as we have seen so often in the battles over wilderness areas, log exports and timber supply."

This observation is not especially controversial. The timber industry and its critics agree that there is no coherent national forest policy. Instead, the forests are the object of a tug of war among competing interests. Their immediate fate in any given locale is determined largely by whoever pulls hardest.

Of course, any national policy that addressed the forests' long-term fate would probably be a compromise among the same interests. It would also be a compendium of educated guesses and wishful thinking. Discussions of forest policy are conducted in definite terms, but they are all based on maybes. Trees take a very long time to mature. If you talk about the life cycle of even an "intensively-managed" forest, you are talking about more time than it takes to plant and harvest a field of corn, more time than it takes to set up a manufacturing process, more time than it takes to design and build a nuclear plant. In fact, you are talking about more time than has elapsed since the start of the space program or the dropping of the Hiroshima bomb. While people may speak with great certainty about what will happen during that cycle or many repetitions of it, the fact is that no one really knows.

7. *Down on the Farm*

During the early 1960s, I often rode a Greyhound bus from Boston to New York, and I frequently found myself rolling through the streets of Harlem on a spring evening. The red neon of a bar or fried-chicken joint flashed in the heavy air, metal grillworks covered the plate glass windows of pawn shops and liquor stores, people milled sweatily on the sidewalks, the shadowy side streets stretched ominously into the night. It always startled me to realize that the land on which those dense, crime-ridden streets stand was once the farming area north of New York. Yet, however startling that realization may have been, the process of urbanization—the expansion of cities onto what was once their farming hinterland—has long seemed both natural and inevitable. New York has sprawled far beyond Harlem. Los Angeles has sprawled through miles of orange groves. Seattle has begun sprawling into the Green River Valley and other fertile areas on its periphery. Portland, Oregon has sprawled into the Willamette Valley. Just as individuals have moved from the farms to the cities, the land itself has moved inexorably away from agricultural use.

Within the past few years, a number of people have come to view the disappearance of agricultural land near cities as a serious national problem and—perhaps more remarkable—as a problem that may be solvable. Their view implies that the use of privately owned land has become a matter of compelling public importance and, as such, a legitimate object of public policy. Philosophically, they have gone a step beyond the argument that forests on *publicly* owned land should be managed for the long-term public good. But they are proceeding from the same basic premise: that private ownership—of land or productive capacity or anything else—should not carry with it the power to deprive society of certain resources or economic options.

The current interest in saving farm land probably owes something to the growth of the environmental movement and also to the originally counter-cultural revival of interest in rural things. It also owes something to political and economic developments of the 1970s. Starvation has become an international issue. As petroleum imports have drained away more and more dollars, food exports have become vital to the United States' balance of payments. Beginning with the Russian wheat deal of 1973, food prices have upset American consumers. The "Green Revolution" has failed to save the less-developed countries from themselves—indeed, in many cases, it seems to have served chiefly to enrich farmers and landowners who were already prosperous. "In parts of the world where population pressure is building," Lester R. Brown has written, "extending food production onto marginal land is already leading to overgrazing, deforestation, desert expansion, soil erosion, silting of irrigation reservoirs, and increased flooding." In the industrial countries, the increased use of fertilizer and machinery on a shrinking land base may have reached the point of diminishing returns. At the beginning of 1977, the Exploratory Project for Economic Alternatives suggested in a widely quoted report that the United States should not only preserve but should expand the farming areas near its cities in order to save some of the energy that must otherwise be used to transport food from distant growing areas.

The former chairman of the California State Assembly's Committee on Resources, Land Use and Energy, Charles Warren, has observed that while "California supplies 25 per cent of all table food and 40 per cent of all fresh vegetables and fruits consumed in the United States, . . . the amount of prime agricultural land in California is shrinking. . . . While our agricultural land base is being balanced by the addition of approximately 55,000 acres of irrigated land per year, this acreage is generally on poorer soils, has lower yields per acre, is more costly to farm per acre and requires a substantially larger energy input (for fertilizer, water transfer and irrigation, farm machinery and transportation) per unit of food production. The California State Division of Soil Conservation has estimated that the total new capital investments to replace converted prime lands is as high as $207 million a year."

In this context, it seems short-sighted to continue paving over naturally fertile soil. Yet the paving still proceeds at a staggering rate. The nation as a whole is losing farm land at the rate of at least a million acres a year. Warren has observed that in his state, "575 acres of prime land are urbanized every day, approximately 21,000 acres each year. . . . Recent studies indicate that in the next decade, prime agricultural land acreage equivalent to the size of the state of Rhode Island will be converted to non-agricultural use. Cities generally expand on land that is flat, accessible, well-drained, favored by climatic conditions—criteria which match exactly those of prime agricultural land."

The reasons for which farm land has disappeared may be complex, but they are not mysterious. One of the least mysterious has been public taxing policy. The Attorney General of California, Evelle J. Younger, has referred to "the impetus which has been given to conversion of prime agricultural land by current [tax] assessment requirements." A familiar pattern in California and elsewhere has been for one or a few tracts of land in an agricultural area to be purchased for development or speculation. The land is worth maybe five times as much for its new or contemplated use as it was for farming. Taxes go up accordingly. But they do not go up only for the plots of land that have been developed or sold. All the land in the area acquires a new "highest and best" use, and everyone's taxes increase five-fold. Farming has generally been a marginal economic operation at best; a five-fold increase in taxes is almost certain death. As more farmers sell out, surrounding municipalities expand into the farm land. They put in roads, utilities and sewers—making it easier than ever to develop the land—and assess the farmers even higher charges to pay for them. And so it goes.

This process has been so clear-cut and so effective that a number of states have now begun to change traditional taxing policy as a logical first step toward halting the erosion of farm land. What they have done is simply set aside the "highest and best" use requirement for assessing agricultural land. Washington State, for example, has passed an Open Space Act that enables a farmer who has actually been working his land to have it assessed at its agricultural value, period. If he sells it or converts it to another use within ten years, he is liable for back taxes at a higher rate.

As a first step, this change in taxing policy is eminently logical. But its impact has been severely limited. It doesn't save the land of a farmer who finds raising berries or onions less attractive than making a killing in real estate. It doesn't save the land of a farmer who looks forward to selling the cow pasture to finance his retirement. It doesn't bring that farmer's children back to the land. It doesn't put stringbeans back onto soil that is no longer being farmed. And it doesn't touch the host of economic problems other than taxes which make the farmer's lot increasingly difficult.

While there has been a growing realization that preserving farmers is as much a part of the ultimate solution as preserving the land, the preservation of land has been much easier to approach, and has consequently been the object of most of the action that has been taken or contemplated by the various interested states.

New York has passed a law that enables a group of landowners to get together and have 500 or more acres of their contiguous holdings declared an agricultural district. Within such a district, taxes must be assessed on the basis of the land's agricultural value, and no extra fees can be assessed for local improvements. Limits are placed on public agencies' power of eminent domain. Municipalities can't shackle farmers with any restrictive ordinances that aren't absolutely necessary to the public health or safety. Any landowner who converts farm land to a use other than agriculture is liable for five years' back taxes at a higher rate. This is a promising system, although some farmers are evidently unhappy with the fact that it prevents them from leaving agriculture without paying an extremely high price.

In California, Assemblyman Warren introduced a bill that would establish a state Agricultural Resources Council and would require a mapping of all prime agricultural land in the state. (Tracts of less than twenty acres would be excluded.) No such land could be removed from agriculture or uses "compatible" with agriculture without the approval of the Council, and then only under certain circumstances. Warren's bill has inevitably drawn opposition—from the California Builders' Council, organized real estate interests and municipalities eager to expand their tax bases, among others—but it has also gathered substantial support. "For too many years," editorialized *The Sacramento Bee,* "the use of California's prime agricultural land has been a real estate version of Russian roulette. To the triumvirate of shortsighted developers, tunnel-visioned industrialists and backroom politicians, the invitation to exploit the foothills, the coast and the rich valleys with little regard for today's problems and tomorrow's needs has been too strong to resist. Warren's bill gives city, county and state officials a way to protect one of California's prime resources."

Legislation that limits the right of private owners to do more or less as they please with private land always arouses hostility. (A perceived threat to private property rights has been one of the main bases of opposition to federal land-use legislation, and presumably the main concern that has brought the right-wing Liberty Lobby into the fray. Traditional zoning upsets people less, perhaps because it has proven notoriously ineffective over the long haul. A regional planning official once summed up the weakness of zoning by saying, "If you get a crackerjack lawyer, you'll eventually get what you want." Faced with a choice between zoning and a form of legislation that is guaranteed to be controversial some government officials have begun looking for new ways out. One of the more promising ways is for the governmental unit itself to acquire legal title to the right to develop the land.

So far, the idea of acquiring development rights has received its greatest exposure in Suffolk County, New York. Located on Long Island, east of New York City, Suffolk has been a farming area since the seventeenth century, and eight Suffolk farms have been worked continuously by the same families since before the Revolution. (One dates from 1661.) The spread of New York City's suburbs has reached Suffolk, however, and it seems clear to some people in the county government that if something isn't done soon, agriculture in the county will be on its way out. They have decided to simply write off the western part of the county, the part closest to New York, where development has gotten the best start and land prices have gone totally out of sight. In the eastern part, they have decided to buy up development rights to 3,883 acres of agricultural land in four townships. The farmer will retain the land itself, but the county government will own the legal right to turn it into anything but field and pasture.

The county could go a step further and just purchase the land, but the current plan seems to offer some advantages. The county will be spared the expense and trouble of getting all the way into the land business. The farmer will still get a big chunk of capital that he can bank or invest for his retirement or use to go out and buy a new tractor. Since he owns the land, he will be able to continue the tradition of the family farm, and he will presumably take a closer interest in his work than he would if he were working the county's land.

The Suffolk County Agricultural Advisory Committee reported to the county legislature in 1974 that the purchase of development rights should be "extremely attractive to legitimate farmers anxious to remain in the agricultural industry in Suffolk County, but hard-pressed by periodic cash shortages and ever-increasing real property taxes, as well as the threat of extensive complications and problems of liquidation upon the death of the farmer. Through the sale of the development rights, he liquidates the greater proportion of his total equity in the value of his real property and converts it to cash which, in turn, can provide him with operating capital, investment capital or income-producing investments. The conversion of the development rights from real property into cash also places the family in a position of avoiding forced liquidation at a sacrifice price at the time of the death of the farmer. . . . Furthermore, the development rights concept provides for the retention of ownership and possession and maintenance of the property with the landowner who, through the pride of ownership and possession can be far more effective in maintaining the physical condition of the property than the county."

The purchase of development rights also has advantages that are strictly political. It placates the ideological defenders of private property by neither taking nor lowering the value of privately owned land without compensation. And it placates speculators and developers by rewarding those who have been holding undeveloped land for speculative gain.

To compute the value of the development rights, Suffolk County has had two appraisals made of the land in question, one to determine its highest market value and one to determine its value if it remains agricultural. The difference between the two equals the value of the development rights. The county has found that in general, development rights are worth 80 per cent of the highest market value of the land.

Whether or not a land-oriented approach, even a land-oriented approach that gives the individual farmer a pile of cash, will suffice to keep that farmer on the land is still most uncertain. Many people believe that guaranteeing the survival of farmland itself will at least go a long way toward solving some of the farmer's other problems. A farmer needs suppliers of equipment and parts, fertilizer and seed, as well as food processing plants and a ready market. Neither suppliers nor processors are likely to stay in, much less enter, an area in which the fields are being paved over without restraint. But if suppliers and processors can be sure that the farm land will be around for many years, they will be likely to stick around, too.

Not that the farmer's problems will be over even then. Making money from the land has always been a complex and risky enterprise, and it has certainly not grown simpler for farmers trying to do it in a region and at a time when agriculture is no longer on many people's minds. "If I go out and hold up a service station," an articulate urban-fringe farmer complained not long ago, "I get more coverage in the [nearby city papers] than if I have a complete crop failure and lose half a million dollars worth of crop." Politicians in urban areas tend to give agricultural problems low priorities. Private citizens tend to give them no priority at all.

The standard view has been, of course, that the small family farm is a kind of relic, that the economic forces impelling the country toward big, corporate farms are irresistible. Actually, beyond a certain point, the economic superiority of sheer size and organizational complexity is far from certain. Many farmers believe that on a farm of a given size, a private owner who has a stake in the land and is willing to work fourteen- and twenty-hour days will outproduce a corporation every time. "Even the Department of Agriculture, which has done much to promote large-scale farming, has published several technical studies which confirm that small farms can be quite efficient," Wilson Clark has written in *Smithsonian*. "The Department's Economic Research Service says that 'the fully mechanized one-man farm, producing the maximum acreage of crops of which the man and his machines are capable, is generally a technically efficient farm. From the standpoint of costs per unit of production, this size farm captures most of the economies associated with size.' Nevertheless, small farms are disappearing daily from the American landscape while corporate farms have become the rule."

There is some question of the minimum size below which a farm simply becomes impractical. Warren's California bill establishes a minimum of 20 acres, and the original version of the bill said 80. The Suffolk County Agricultural Advisory Committee suggested to the county legislature that "the preserved farms should . . . constitute relatively large tracts, preferably a minimum of 200 acres in size. Preservation of individual isolated farms would not be conducive to continued agricultural operation on them. Preserved farms should be bounded to the maximum extent possible by existing roads or highways, or other open spaces, so as to provide for a buffer or insulation zone between the farm activity and other nearby residential or commercial uses."

At what point do farms or farming areas cease to be worth saving? Do the marketing problems of small farmers stem from immutable economic laws or from the buying policies of profit-hungry grocery chains? What about the farms in a place like the urbanizing valleys around Seattle? A King County, Washington councilman named Mike Lowry, who represents some of Seattle's farming hinterland, answers that such farms are still well worth saving—that within King County, they still generate some $40 million a year. In Suffolk County, New York, agriculture still generates some $80 million a year.

Even assuming that farming in urban areas is still a viable industry and not merely an aesthetic amenity, there seems no reasonable doubt that at least some of the current interest in saving it stems from a romantic image of the small farmer. It would be easy but myopic to attribute this romanticism entirely to a reaction against mid-twentieth-century technology and urbanism, to consider it simply another facet of the back-to-the-country and organic gardening movements or an offshoot of the same bizarre impulse that a few years ago sent hip young New Yorkers strolling down Fifth Avenue wearing unsullied bib overalls above their platform shoes.

Actually, this country has harbored a romantic view of rural life for most of its 200-odd years. As the late Richard Hofstadter observed in *The Age of Reform,* "The American was taught throughout the nineteenth and even the twentieth century that rural life and farming as a vocation were something sacred." From the very beginning, Hofstadter wrote, "the articulate people were drawn irresistibly to the noncommercial, nonpecuniary, self-sufficient aspect of American farm life. . . . The American mind was raised upon a sentimental attachment to rural living and upon a series of notions about rural people and rural life that I have chosen to designate as the agrarian myth. . . . Oddly enough, the agrarian myth came to be believed more widely and tenaciously as it became more fictional."

It was always somewhat fictional, Hofstadter argued, and rapidly became more so. " 'My farm,' said the farmer of Jefferson's time, 'gave me and my family a good living on the produce of it; and left me, one year with another, one hundred and fifty silver dollars, for I have never spent more than ten dollars a year, which was for salt, nails and the like. Nothing to wear, eat or drink was purchased, as my farm provided all. With this saving, I put money to interest, bought cattle, fatted and sold them, and made great profit.' Here, then, was the significance of self-sufficiency for the characteristic family farmer: 'great profit.' "

The profits came both from specializing in a cash crop and from speculating in land. "Between 1815 and 1860," Hofstadter wrote, "the character of American agriculture was transformed. The independent yeoman, outside of exceptional or isolated areas, almost disappeared before the relentless advance of commercial agriculture. . . . The shift from self-sufficiency to commercial farming . . . was complete in Ohio by about 1830 and twenty years later in Indiana, Illinois and Michigan." The completion of the Erie Canal, which provided a cheap, quick way of transporting produce from the Midwest to the East, also brought an end to the great period of yeoman farming in much of New England. In a study of the old Moon farm in Williamstown, Massachusetts, Richard F. Olivo and Henry W. Art wrote in the November, 1975 issue of *Natural History* that "as agricultural competition from the Midwest forced a shift from subsistence farming to larger, specialized commercial farms, and as manufacturing rose in New England, farming declined. By 1850, farm abandonment had reduced the open land in Williamstown to about 50 per cent. . . . Thus by the late 1850s, when Daniel Moon, Alfred's father, bought the farm, it had already become an anachronism; it was a small, hillside subsistence farm in an era when many small farms had been abandoned or consolidated into larger sheep and dairy farms."

Since the earliest days of the nation, as Hofstadter pointed out, it was possible to profit not only from the products of the land, but also from the land itself. "Already in the late eighteenth century," he observed, "writers on American agriculture noticed that American farmers were tempted to buy more land than they could properly cultivate. . . . In 1818, the English immigrant Morris Birback wrote from Illinois that "the farmer, instead of completing the improvement of his present possessions, lays out all he can save in entering more land. In a district which is settling, this speculation is said to pay on the average, when managed with judgment, fifteen per cent.' . . . Frequent and sensational rises in land values bred a boom psychology in the American farmer and caused him to rely for his margin of profit more on the process of appreciation than on the sale of crops. . . . What developed in America was an agricultural society whose real attachment was not to the land but to land values."

Hofstadter overstated his case, as debunkers tend to do. Certainly, there have been and still are a great many American farmers who like their work and their life, whose primary attachment has never been to speculation in land. Certainly, there are many Americans alive today who acquired an impressive range of skills and a formidable capacity for hard work by growing up on farms that approximated the romantic image of self-reliance. Still, Hofstadter's basic point is well taken, and must be considered in any rational attempt to preserve small-scale agriculture or agriculture on any scale along the urban periphery. Farming is above all an economic enterprise. The farmer must make a living and prefers to make a healthy profit. Sometimes he prefers to make an out-and-out killing, which in many cases he can do most easily by selling his land. This is not a sign of modern corruption, a product of pressures unique to the mid-twentieth century; it is the nature of the farming business. And farming is a business.

Preserving the urban-area farm is less like saving the bald eagle than like preserving the mom-and-pop grocery. It isn't simply a matter of putting up no-hunting signs and banning the sale of feathers; it requires altering a complex economic and social system. The people who want to save small farms in urban areas can't do much about the high prices farmers must pay for equipment, fuel and fertilizer. But would they be willing to pay higher food prices so that the farmer could get a greater rate of return on his investment of cash and labor? Would they support taxes that penalized grocery chains which rejected local farm products in order to buy in greater bulk from distant corporate farms? Would they be willing to set aside the child labor laws that make it hard to get berry pickers, the housing laws that make it hard for small farmers to employ seasonal migrant labor, the social-welfare payments that evidently make low-paying temporary work on farms less attractive than it once was to low-income segments of society? Whether or not they should be willing to do such things is at best an open question, but it is the kind of question that must at least be addressed if one is to deal seriously with the problems of farmers on the urban fringe.

No one ever decided to phase out farms on the peripheries of cities. Many decisions were made which had that effect, but they were never intended to have that effect. Governments, hard pressed to fund growing numbers of programs and support growing numbers of employees, decided to maximize their tax revenues. Entrepreneurs, faced with relatively cheap land and expanding populations, made the logical decision to build houses and shopping centers on the land. Home buyers, who wanted individual houses and yards not in, but not too far from the cities, decided to move into areas that used to be farms. Businesses, finding sites that were close to roads, railroads and workers but less expensive and less heavily taxed than city property, decided to move there, too. Utility companies, anticipating population booms in those areas, sensibly decided to beat the rush and installed the services that made booms possible. Reformers, seeing the often-brutal conditions under which farm laborers worked and lived, decided to press for laws that would increase their wages, improve their living conditions, keep children out of the fields. Farmers and the children of farmers, not relishing the prospect of a lifetime of fourteen, sixteen, eighteen-hour days, preferring urban incomes and urban social opportunities, decided to leave the land, rationally selling it to the highest bidder. The indirect effect of all these perfectly reasonable decisions has been the looming extinction of a certain kind of farm.

To reverse the currents that are sweeping those farms into history—if, indeed, the currents can be reversed—society can't rely on further indirection. Instead, society will have to decide explicitly that the farms should be saved—that the metropolitan landscape and the metropolitan table should not be further impoverished, that the nation should not try to feed itself by continually applying more energy to less land—and then take explicit steps to save them.

8. The Absence of Buffalo

SEVERAL years ago, my wife and I went to visit her late grandfather in the small farming village in central Utah around which he had spent his life. The valley in which the village lies is arid, requiring irrigation to raise any kind of crop. (Four years earlier, when my grandfather-in-law was eighty, he had complained that he was fit only for driving tractors and building small cattle sheds because as a young man, riding horseback along the irrigation canals for forty-eight hours at a stretch, he had wrecked his health.) The surrounding hills are equally dry, a parched, tawny backdrop to the valley floor.

Both I and my wife, who spent her childhood in the valley, assumed that the hills had always looked like that, that their stark outlines had greeted the first white settlers in 1856. Not so, my grandfather-in-law said; he could remember when they were covered with grass that grew waist-high, when you could stand there in the valley and see the herds of wild horses moving down through the grass. What had happened, he said, was that every spring, the sheepherders had driven their flocks up into the hills right behind the receding snow. As each year's new grass had poked through the soil, the sheep had eaten it down to the roots. What they hadn't eaten, they had trampled into the spring mud. After enough years of that, they had created a desert.

The impact of the sheepherders and their flocks may not have been permanent—the grass seems to be coming back—but it is staggering nevertheless. And history is full of such chance human revisions of the earth. Nobody expects to see flocks of passenger pigeons or great herds of buffalo again, and most people don't even know that much of the Midwest was once covered with hardwood forests, or that New England's rivers were once choked with salmon.

There is something both awesome and sinister about things that can do harm far out of proportion to their size: the power of the snake or the bullet is somehow more chilling than the power of the tiger or the club, the power of the germ or the ionizing ray the most chilling of all. It is similarly awesome and perhaps similarly chilling that mankind, chained to its Biblical threescore years and ten, can leave footprints that last for eons.

Yet man has done and continues to do so, sometimes by accident and sometimes by design. One of the main objections to the development of nuclear power has been that plutonium, which virtually all reactors produce and which breeder reactors can use as fuel, requires some 100,000 years to lose even half its radioactivity. Radiation from the plutonium waste that this generation plans to create could, in theory, cause enough genetic damage to permanently alter the human gene pool. Some proponents of nuclear power have dismissed this objection out of hand, suggesting that radiation is just one of the thousands of risks that mankind has had to live with, and that like other risks, it can undoubtedly be overcome.

Yet thoughtful people have always felt that there is something unusual and disconcerting about radiation, that when mankind gained the ability and the will to manipulate it, we crossed a historical threshold. "The force was wholly new,"

Henry Adams wrote from the perspective of 1900. ". . . the nearest approach to the revolution of 1900 [actually, Wilhelm Roentgen had discovered x-rays in 1895, and Marie Curie had discovered radium in 1898] was that of 310, when Constantine set up the Cross. The rays . . . were occult, supersensual, irrational; they were a revelation of mysterious energy like that of the Cross; they were what, in terms of medieval science, were called immediate modes of the divine substance."

Alvin M. Weinberg, former director of the Oak Ridge National Laboratory, who has been one of the most dedicated advocates of nuclear energy but also one of the most philosophical, readily concedes that the long-lasting nature of radioactive wastes is something unique, something that can't simply be argued away. A commitment to store those wastes for even a fraction of their 100,000-year-half-lives, he once told me, "presupposes a kind of eerie institutional stability." The only similar commitment he could think of, he said, was Hitler's instruction to his architect to choose building materials that would last through the full lifetime of the Thousand Year Reich.

Implicit in the nation's recent concern with energy and the environment has been that same gnawing awareness of time—or perhaps not of time but of eternity. It is one thing to suppose that the blue whale or the wolf or the peregrine falcon will disappear for a few years. It is quite another to suppose that the world will be without wolves or peregrine falcons or blue whales forever. Likewise, it is the prospect of using up petroleum or having to store radioactive wastes, not just for a while, but forever that makes the debates over energy so momentous in the minds of the debaters.

A sense of permanence—or the fact of permanence—also lies at the heart of virtually all the conflicts over resources. This is not exactly the same as a sense of time. Time is the medium in which all the supply curves and demand curves can intersect. It is also the medium through which the hare-and-tortoise race between the planned and unplanned effects of current decisions will be run.

But economically and psychologically, the crux of the matter is not just time but irreversibility: the fact or the sense that over the lifetime of the earth or human civilization or a given society, things will be irrevocably different because of decisions and acts performed now. If it were possible to fish out a salmon run or pave over a fertile valley now, when the pressure is intense and the price is right, and then be sure of having more fish or fertile soil in a few years, the loss might be relatively trivial. But if the destruction of fish or farm land or other resources must be protected over generations or centuries—or the whole foreseeable future of civilization—the loss becomes immense.

The point is not that mankind should stop exploiting the natural resources that surround it. People who really live "close to nature"—the members of a hunting society or an agricultural society—live in a direct economic relationship with nature. In an industrial or "post-industrial" society, individuals may lose that direct economic relationship, but the society as a whole does not. The individual may consider the relationship sordid, but society as a whole would not survive without it.

If society kept its hands to itself, nature would not automatically provide for all human needs. At this stage of history, nature simply can't provide for all human needs. And nature has never provided for more than a few of them without intense human effort. Agriculture has always been hard work; hunting and gathering have seldom been an easy or secure way to fill one's stomach.

We do not have the option of sitting back and letting the fruits of the earth fall into our open mouths. But we may have the options of preserving or destroying a world in which the fruits are at least readily available. We may have the choice of saddling or not saddling our descendants with a world in which nature hardly provides at all, a world in which great efforts must be made to sustain a cumbersome economic system that was created by the short-term opportunism of the past. We may be able to leave our portion of the natural world as a more or less hospitable place.

Whether or not future generations would curse us for our choice is hardly the point. The absence of salmon or truck farms or red cedar is the kind of thing that people may regret if they think about it, but that no one will really see, and that few are likely to consider from one year to the next. One does not, after all, actively notice the absence of buffalo.

The people of the future who must wrestle with the shortages that this generation creates will probably be too absorbed by the wrestling to waste much time on might-have-beens. Yeats wrote in *Lapis Lazuli* that,

> All things fall and are built again,
> And those that build them again are gay.

He was talking about civilizations, but the point is still well taken: builders enjoy building. The process of building absorbs people. If one is absorbed by the process of building, one may not pause long to regret the necessity of building.

One may also reflect little on the negative consequences of building. It is unlikely that even knowing the long-term consequences of their acts, our own forebears would have acted differently. Would they have turned their backs on the Industrial Revolution in order to save the New England salmon? Would they have abandoned their effort to turn the Midwest into farm land if they had realized that forests of the kind they were cutting and burning would never be seen again? In some cases they might have been willing to alter their course, but in most cases, they probably would not. And in fact, all things considered, we might not have wanted them to act differently.

Still, one's view of the present is necessarily different from one's view of the past. Whether or not we would prefer to have been spared the Industrial Revolution is hardly the question. History has an air of inevitability about it. The choices of the present—which are the routes to the future— do not. If they did, we wouldn't see them as choices.

There is very little choice, actually, about the nature of the people and institutions that will exploit the resources of this continent in the present and the future. They are the people and institutions in a position to profit from the use of those resources. They have the capital and the technical means to use them. And they have the initiative. In chess, the initiative is hard to define but almost palpable. A player with fewer pieces than his opponent can gain and hold the initiative, and everyone who understands the game will know he has it. Gaining the initiative in chess requires the opportunity and the will to act, and some sense of what to do—either a long-range plan or immediate step-by-step objectives. To gain the initiative in the use of natural resources, one needs similar things: a perceived opportunity for gain, the will to exploit that opportunity and some idea of how to exploit it.

The possession of initiative, capital and technology may not qualify anyone in a moral or intellectual sense to determine the future of natural resources, but it certainly empowers people to do so. To limit their power, one must place a coun- tervailing power in the hands of the state—which, except for revolution, is the only form in which society can act. If a resource such as the Pacific salmon falls partly or wholly out- side the jurisdiction of some form of the state, then society, as represented by that particular state, is not able to control its use. The prospect of placing more power in the hands of any state may not be attractive, but then, neither is the alter- native.

For individuals or corporations, the prospect of society's fu- ture loss may easily be outweighed by the prospect of their own present gain. It may, in fact, be quite rational for anyone to make a lot of money right now, at the expense of future generations. But whether or not individuals are willing to sacrifice for the sake of their descendants, society has a stake in assuring for itself a certain kind of future.

If an individual tries to approach the future prudently— decides to put his money in the bank instead of blowing it in Las Vegas, or decides not to cut down his best apple tree for firewood—no one gets very upset. If society tries to be prudent, some people get very upset indeed. The difference is that while prudence requires an individual to choose among competing impulses, it requires a society to choose among competing individuals—or groups or generations—and somebody's ox is sure to be gored.

How society should make that kind of choice and within what limits it should be made are extremely tricky questions. They may not be questions to which anyone can provide fully satisfactory answers. The more one moves from generalities to specifics, the trickier they become. It is easy to philosophize that society's resources should be used prudently. It is not easy to say that the prudent use of this hundred acres should be defined by society—possibly represented by some unelected, well-paid and securely pensioned bureaucrat —and not by the person who has bought and paid for it. But unless society does define prudence, albeit within stringent limits, the future will be up for grabs—or will be shaped piecemeal by the economic decisions of those who have already grabbed. Of course, that may simply be the nature of futures.

Index